NAKED AMBITION

NAKED AMBITION

My Quest to Row an Ocean

Richard Wood

Victory Books

Dedication

To my father, Lionel James Wood, 1912-2003.
"Giving up wasn't an option".
&
for my mother, Margaret Walton Wood.
"Still alive & kicking!"

NAKED AMBITION: My Quest to Row an Ocean.

© Richard Wood, 2006.
ISBN: 0-9550431-7-4

First published 2006 by Victory Books, PO Box 573, Worcester WR5 3WU
Tel: 07921 503105. Fax: 01905 767735. Web: www.victorybooks.co.uk.

Design & layout by Victory Books. Printed & bound in the UK.

Contents

Acknowledgements

Many people, organisations and businesses came together and helped me to achieve my ambition: -

- My wife Usha and children Nayna, John & Joshua for their consistent long suffering support and encouragement.
- My sister Alison and brother in law Richard whose generous financial support helped keep things afloat!
- My mother Margaret who, apart from being the best Mum I've got, was generous enough to help this book project with a loan.
- Rob Ringer, whose friendship I value very highly despite all the traumas.
- Therese, Paul and Zoe Ringer for their support of the row.
- Al, Rob and the other volunteers who helped with the boat build in Appleby.
- Kenneth & Tatiana Crutchlow founders of the Ocean Rowing Society. I count them as valued friends and the 'President & First Lady of Ocean Rowing'!
- Dave Cave for his consistent practical and financial help and his admiration and belief in me that has been a constant source of encouragement.
- Barney Price, Jeanie Young and all the team at St Richard's Hospice Worcester for their hard work support and enthusiasm without which the project would have been much the poorer.
- Alby McCracken my good friend in Oz and world expert on all things to do with Para anchors, don't go to sea without one!
- Mary Jenks & Angela Hughes for taking my first contact at St Richard's seriously!
- Doug and Anita Carroll my good friends in La Gomera who came to my assistance at the end of the first attempt and gave me Dougan at the start of the second. (Not forgetting crewmember Neil)
- Dilip and Anita Sakar at Victory Books for their expertise and enthusiasm for the book project.
- James, Gareth, Anna & Josie our sports science Phd team at University College Chester Sports Science Department for putting up with hours in the lab and all that urine, sweat and blood!
- Paul Weighton manager at Cannons Health Club in Worcester where I had free membership for a number of years and all the subsequent managers who agreed to its continuation.
- Richard Lovell and the Team at Arena for their exceptional commitment to the marketing of the challenge.
- Brian Saunders and the support of the Inland Waterways Association at the 1999 Festival in Worcester.
- Trevor Lloyd Adams Crowngate Centre Manager for sponsoring the trailer and giving inspiration for the boat name.
- Dr Mike Duke from Southbank University and his Team for the provision and installation of all our solar power needs.
- Sven from the solar team who came out to El Hierro to deliver and install my Sat phone for the first solo attempt.

- My Youth Service work mates Bridget Cooper, Paul Finnemore, Adrian Newman and the Youthcomm Team and special thanks to Lesley Butcher for her loyalty and hard work.
- Worcestershire County Council for being such understanding and long suffering employers.
- Phil, Tony, David and all the Team at Checketts the butchers of Ombersley for their consistent support, encouragement, enthusiasm & jolly good Biltong!
- Chris Spears and his Discovery plus all those airport trips!
- Babette Moreau and her fantastic help and hospitality in our hour of need in El Hierro.
- My mate Graham Coyle for all the help and support of the River School and its facilities not forgetting Mike for being so helpful and patient with my constant requests during the refit.
- Paul McGonagle with his fantastic solar installation on Najojo.
- Stein, Diana Hoff and Eli for their kind hospitality on board White Admiral in La Gomera before the race start (time Diana got her MBE me thinks!)
- Peter Hogden and his crew, Phil & Johan for their support on Kilcullen.
- Bob Barnsley our ORS scrutineer for his good natured support for all us rowers.
- Mike Lapac and his team at Universal Display Ltd then Signworx for his boat branding expertise.
- Louis Ginglo as a fellow solo rower for his friendship and company prior to the race.
- Tim Woodman from the University of Wales for his sports psychology support
- Frank at George Judge Chandlery Worcester for all those extra bits and help.
- Matt Murfitt for his hospitality and help on the Isle of Man and Kerry Bladin on Jersey.
- James and the Worcester Standard Team
- Sundeep Kumar & The Worcester Evening News
- BBC Hereford & Worcester
- BBC Midlands Today & Central TV
- The Birmingham Post
- Appleby Heritage Centre for their help with providing a place and equipment to build the Spirit of Worcestershire.
- Upton Warren Sailing Centre for the use of their facilities.
- All the assistance offered by Pitchcroft Boating Station and their chandlery before it closed.
- Sealine International for providing boat building materials and GPS units.
- International Coatings for all our paint requirements.
- Automatic Packaging Worcester for making the stainless steel rudder fittings.
- BP for the provision of tailor made survival suits and a life raft especially Helana Peterson who arranged it all.

And finally everyone who gave to the project in every way, showed their support, gave to St Richard's and generally made the project happen......THANK YOU!

Foreword

It was in 1998 when the call came through from our Fund Raising Manager: "I have just been speaking to this chap who wants to raise money for our new Hospice … by rowing across the Atlantic. Do you want to see him?" Not every day do we at St Richard's Hospice receive such an offer and so we grappled for a suitable response. What an opportunity! What a worry! What happens if he sinks? Is the Hospice liable, are we personally liable, who is this man and, indeed, is he of sound mind?

So started the long and close ties between St Richard's Hospice and Richard Wood, and in those early days his friend, fellow rower Rob Ringer. That first meeting really told us all, as we met a man who wore his heart on his sleeve, driven by this courageous yet outrageous ambition, utterly convinced of its ultimate success and equally convincing as he spelt out his case. So far as we could see, Richard also appeared completely sane!

Looking back now, through this book's draft manuscript, it is strange how fading recollections become vivid once more. Transatlantic crossings by rowing boat have perhaps become more commonplace in recent times, increasingly attracting the multi-media hype, but it seemed so very different then. The folk who did these rows then were, by and large, quite ordinary, set on their own and very private mission, and largely unsung as they achieved their greatest goal in life. Records show that Richard was the 11th person to row solo on the route he took, spending over 100 days along the way; but that was just the final stage of an epic journey that lasted several years and tested him, his tenacity, ingenuity, his family and friends to the full – long before ever Richard sat at the oars of 'Najojo' in Gomera harbour. The story is, in fact, a great example to us all of what can be achieved by self-belief, sacrifice and dogged determination… and red meat enough for most.

To us, the fact that a safe landing at the Barbados destination would always be a struggle was part of the appeal. This was a personal tale. All sorts of mind games would be required along the way, the setbacks were likely to be daunting, and so they proved, and many would have to be faced alone. There were parallels with our Hospice's patients, who never cease to amaze with their fortitude, resilience and unbending spirit. These qualities were a large part of Richard's inspiration as he set about his enterprise, now with the added weight upon his shoulders of our Hospice's expectations. Later this role would be reversed as the daily progress of this dot across the massive ocean was eagerly plotted in our Day Hospice's lounge, willed on y those who knew a thing or two about a daily struggle.

On another level this is a story of money and how to raise it, spend it and still have fun. In some small way we helped contribute to Richard's project by doing things together. In return he vowed to see us right. His budget to build and equip his boat was £35,000, a frightening prospect; ours to build and equip a brand new Hospice for Worcester was £5.25 million. If nothing else, Richard is competitive and from that standing start it became clear who was likely to get there first. Richard made his landfall on April 30th, 2004, job done. 21 months later, on January 30th, 2006, we announced having made it too. Into our pot went the thousands of pounds that Richard had attracted on his own through sponsorship and media coverage, a huge boost to our funds and local awareness.

Once in a while things happen that bring new dimension and excitement to our lives. We were very pleased to receive Richard's initial call, sweeping us, as it did, into situations we'd not been in before. The Hospice was privileged to share the trials and tribulations, moments of great pleasure and relief, which is the stuff of all that follows in this book. Life is richer for the adventurer and that he certainly is. Knowing some of the cast, as it were, and the roles they played brings extra personal pleasure; these are real people who, for the most part, are doing regular jobs but were, for a while, vital to the linked events that made Richard's Atlantic crossing possible. His company, *The Spirit of Worcestershire*, set up to run the operation, is now wound up. It was a single-purpose company for a single-minded man, a chapter that is now closed. It's all too easy to buy another off the shelf, should the need arise, and who's to say it won't?

It has been an honour to write these few words, about an extraordinary man and his wonderfully devoted family, for whom our praise is boundless. Thank you, Richard for adding colour to our lives. Congratulations on your great achievement and this superb account of your Atlantic Row.

Barney Price, St Richard's Hospice, Worcester, February 2nd, 2006

Introduction

Richard

I have just caught up with your website with some help from Jack. The best stories are often those where the action does not come easily, where there are considerable trials, physical, mental and emotional, as well as competition and the big challenge of crossing the Atlantic. You have such a tale and it was an absorbing and gripping read for us all. Much more interesting than straight forward success. Your sense of commitment and determination are very tangible and together with Usha's impressive support I would call it a brilliant effort - so well done - I'm inspired! I feel that there is a bit of the ghost of Shackleton here but perhaps I am going on already to much!

Kind regards
John

Much water has passed beneath the proverbial bridge since 1972, when John and I landed in Bahrain to join the MS *Manora* a general cargo ship of the P&O Line. We were 16-years old and part of a group of eight deck cadets looking forward to a life at sea with the hope of commanding our own vessels over distant horizons someday in the future. After nearly a year on the Australia-Persian Gulf run and many adventures, we flew back to the UK from Muscat to begin the first part of our shore based training in Plymouth. Both John and I subsequently left the merchant navy and lost contact. Nearly 30 years later John got in touch again just prior to my trans-Atlantic rowing challenge. I received his note on my return and it reflects the overwhelming and somewhat humbling support from so many people, who for some reason found our attempt a great inspiration.

There is a great British tradition of love for the underdog, for those who strive to meet their chosen challenge, whatever form it may take, and give it their best shot even if they fail to achieve the ultimate goal. Ernest Shackleton is one of my all time heroes and his adventure is one of the best known examples of making history whilst completely failing to achieve what he set out to do. Despite John's allusion to the great explorer, in no way would I presume to come anywhere close to his epic journey. I do however recognise that he dared to step out into the unknown, had faith in his ability to succeed and when he failed to achieve his ambition remained undaunted, turning his attention to the safety of his fellow explorers and the new challenge that faced him. It is this kind of commitment, determination and bravery tempered with realism and compassion that strikes a cord in people's hearts.

In 1998 I embarked on a journey that failed to achieve what I set out to do, but I would not be beaten and was determined not to give up. This narrative recounts the story of that journey, the milestones I passed, the people I met, the unexpected impact it made on so many lives and the ultimate outcome of many years of dedication and hard work. I invite you to join me and relive my great Atlantic Adventure as it unfolds in the pages to come. This book is a labour of love dedicated to you and all those who have helped me so far. The tide is now turning as I look to a new horizon in preparation for the ultimate rowing challenge.

Richard Wood, Worcester, January 2006.
www.rowextreme.com

Chapter One

I was inspired. It was Christmas 1997, and for several weeks I had been following the progress of the first Atlantic Rowing Race on the Internet. I can't remember where I originally found out about the challenge but I downloaded the daily reports and was fascinated, not only by the progress of the international teams involved but also their motivation for embarking on such an adventure.

A few months prior to the start I had written to the race organisers and asked if I could participate. I realise, in the light of subsequent experience, the naïveté of that request as there was no way that I'd have had time to put together such a complex project in such a short space of time. They did say, however, that I could go on the waiting list, and once an evaluation of the race had taken place and a positive decision made to organise another one, I could apply for registration on a first come first served basis. The irresistible prospect of becoming involved grabbed my attention and I made up my mind this was a challenge made for me.

I had gone to sea at 16 to train as a Deck Cadet with the P&O General Cargo Division. Prior to this I had made several sailing trips to continental Europe with the Ocean Youth Club. There was no tradition of the sea in my family, but I felt like the sea was in my blood. However, after nearly two years of both sea and shore based training I decided on a different direction for my life: I left, going back to my parent's home in Kent to decide what might come next.

I then met an old friend of mine who was planning to go to Australia to train and work. His intention was to do the trip overland by public transport and I volunteered to keep him company! It was June 1976, Canon Chapman's, Westerham High Street Boogy Woogy Band played it's last gig on a farm trailer in a field just outside the town. I played guitar and sang. A gentle drizzle formed droplets on the tarpaulin we rigged over the trailer for such eventualities but unfortunately its waterproof capabilities were lacking, causing some 'collateral damage' as the drips fell from above to tease our electrical equipment! This event remains in my memory, as it was the last rain that would be seen in the UK until September and marked the beginning of the great drought of 1976.

MS Manora.

The author working aboard MS Manora, aged 16.

60 feet waves in the Great Australian Bight.

The author on the Channel ferry, beginning a memorable journey.

The next day we said farewell to our families at Dover and boarded a ferry for Calais, on what was the first leg of a long and eventful trip, taking us by ship, train, bus and plane across France and northern Italy, down through Yugoslavia and Bulgaria, into Turkey and some of the most frightening mountain roads I have ever experienced. Actually it wasn't that the roads that were particularly frightening, it was the people using them! Our bus driver appeared to have a death wish, or may be he was just keen to be martyred, unfortunately he hadn't informed his passengers of this before departure but in retrospect perhaps there is some truth in the saying, 'ignorance is bliss'! It was our first encounter with Turkish bus and lorry drivers' mountain road craft. This entailed sounding an extremely loud two tone horn whilst approaching and negotiating horrendously sharp blind bends, flanked on one side by sheer rock walls and on the other by sheer drops, and at the bottom of which lay the remains of various vehicles that had failed to fly! Presumably, the object of the exercise was to warn drivers of other buses or lorries coming in the opposite direction to ourselves. The only trouble with this strategy was that the driver coming the other way had a

Our intrepid author, having survived a lift from a one-armed driver!

similarly deafening two toner that he was just as keen to use and obviously felt the same right of road ownership as our driver! Fortunately there was just enough room for two vehicles to pass, but only just; all we could do was hang on and pray. The scenery was fantastic, however, and if you could re-focus your eyes from a stare of vacant terror through the front windscreen the rewards were spectacular.

After the rigours of Turkish mountain roads, Istanbul provided some light relief, especially our visit to the Blue Mosque where Richard, my travelling companion, got vociferously sworn at by a mosque 'minder' whose only English is unprintable and thought, as many of us do, that if a foreigner doesn't understand you because he doesn't speak the language, all you have to do is shout louder and louder and eventually the penny will drop! The reason for his outburst had something to do with shoes, we had removed ours, as is the traditional mark of respect when entering a mosque but we must have put them in the wrong place or something. Whilst avoiding the wrath of God the 'minder' was obviously not in the mood to show mercy. We moved the shoes and our new acquaintance went off to persecute some other unsuspecting tourist, leaving us to enjoy the rest of the visit to this majestic building.

Another bus took us on to Iran where a queue of lorries several miles long were waiting up to two weeks to cross the border. Fortunately our driver ignored this and we left Turkey after a couple of hours of formalities. There were three crew on our bus journey from Istanbul, a steward and two drivers, One driver would sleep in a bed at the back of the bus whilst the other drove ever onward. They would alternate every so often but both were keen fans of traditional Iranian music. The whole point of the trip was to mix with the locals and enjoy a snapshot of their culture, but these constant strains began to get to me. Occasionally the music would change to something more familiar but he would quickly re-tune the radio to another Iranian top 20 station. I was slowly driven mad and you can imagine my relief when we finally made our next hotel. My joy was short lived, though, when the occupant of the next room sent the cockroaches scuttling as he played more Iranian hits on his ghetto blaster. It was all too much; I just wanted sleep so drastic action was required. I took some toilet tissue and stuffed it in my ears. It worked, but the next day I was unable to extract the offending material from one side. I asked Richard to help and he used the top of his biro to try and dig it out. Unfortunately he only managed to push it deeper and compact it into my head. On arrival in the next major city, Tehran, I made my way from the hotel to the British Embassy to find a doctor who could help. What I hadn't been told was in Tehran green traffic lights mean go and a red one means go even faster; I could only deduce that the Tehranians had been to the same driving school as our Turkish bus driver, or perhaps he had made a video! Once you got the hang of it, however, your life expectancy was considerably increased. I made it to the Embassy and told the doctor of my predicament, which seemed to cause him a great deal of amusement rather than the up welling of deep sympathy I was expecting. He picked up a large pair of tongs and jammed them into my ear extracting the paper in one deft and extremely painful manoeuvre. I felt a great sense of relief, particularly as I could hear again.

Iran gave way to Afghanistan where I contracted 'Dehli Belly' although in this case it was 'Herat Belly', which doesn't rhyme so well, but the effects are the same. This ailment did help us, in fact, as the next bus, bound for Kabul, left at 0400 hours and we would probably have missed it if I hadn't been constantly seeking refuge in the toilet! Speaking of which, the bus would occasionally stop at roadside cafes for passengers to purchase refreshments and have a stretch, but the condition of these establishments would have caused an environmental health officer to weep. This was underlined when I asked a local where the toilet was, "Ahhh" he replied, brandishing a hand in the general direction of the surrounding desert, "Afghanistan one great toilet!" With that I retired to the back of the building and the rest is history!

As we crossed the desert one of the great mysteries of the country unfolded. A small black dot appeared on the horizon and as it came nearer revealed an individual beside the road with an insulated box full of ice and Coke, this was of course pre Taliban, just before the Russian invasion, but miles from anywhere; it begs the question, where did he get the Coke from let alone the ice? It will forever remain a mystery to me!

Having said that, we found the people very friendly and concerned for our welfare, particularly when they found out I was feeling pretty rough. It was extremely hot and dehydration was a bit of a problem. An Afghan travelling with us on the bus told me not to drink the water, not just because of our lack of capacity as Europeans to fight off water born bugs but the danger to any traveller who dared to risk fighting dehydration with raw water. This was clearly demonstrated when another Afghan had died on a bus the previous week from a water related illness. So the Coke bloke turned out to be a bit of a lifesaver!

Talking of Coke, after we had rested a while in Kabul we set out for the Pakistan Border. This was a part of the trip I was looking forward to, as we had to go through the Khyber Pass. It reminds me of the first time I went to Northern Ireland before the cease fire, passing through places that I had only heard about on the news and suddenly you are experiencing them for yourself. The Pass is the stuff of history and the area around it remains run by local tribal leaders. Those you did see carried Lee Enfield .303 rifles, with belts of ammunition slung across their shoulders making a large X over their chests. We were told a smugglers' train came up the pass every week from Peshawar and buses were often stopped and the occupants robbed. Fortunately we avoided such a scenario and made it to the border. The vendors openly selling various drugs from biscuit tins by the road amazed us, but we declined their special offers and headed for Lahore.

We crossed Pakistan, entered India and travelled by train to Calcutta. The visit to this amazing city was quite an eye opener: abject poverty side by side with considerable wealth. India is a land of contrasts and completely different to the culture we are used to in the UK, which made our short stay of particular interest. We left by plane, as the political situation in Burma at the time did not allow us to do this leg overland. The train from Bangkok took us through the jungle from Thailand into Malaysia. The journey was marked by 40 American Mormons on board whose mission, apart from travelling to the border to renew their visas, appeared to be to convince us that "Joseph Smith was a true prophet of Gaad"; as I couldn't remember anyone by the name of Smith in the Bible I remained unconvinced, not bad for a 20:1, missionary: victim ratio! Anyway if things had got really bad, I could have called on the heavily armed guards carrying machine-guns and grenades who accompanied the train in case of bandit attack!

We made it to Penang and were advised that the route down through Sumatra was very dangerous. With my shipboard experience I went to the port in Medan and found a small coastal vessel on passage to Jakarta. For a small fee the Chief Officer agreed to relinquish his cabin for us and supply food. This seemed a good deal so we gladly accepted and had a very pleasant trip down to our last port of call before flying over to Oz.

After a couple of eventful weeks in Western Australia I said an emotional farewell to Richard who had been such an excellent travelling companion and all round good bloke. A fact that my sister Alison obviously agreed with when she subsequently married him! I flew back to the UK and was staggered by the state of the country as we began our descent into Heathrow. Instead of England's green and pleasant land stretching out below, there was an alien scene of barren brown hues the result of three months baking without a drop of rain, as it was coming to the end of the great drought of 1976.

As the plane touched down I had a real sense of achievement, albeit tinged with unrest, an emotion I have become all to familiar with over the years. It's a fleeting sense of completeness mixed with a real desire to move on. This can be frustrating if the next challenge is as yet ill defined or non existent, but I know that if I can stay with it, and weather these interludes, something will be waiting round the corner to grab my energies.

The journey, like my time at sea and the trips with the Ocean Youth Club had given me a taste for adventure, a thirst for challenge and a desire to take others with me. I also thoroughly enjoyed meeting so many different people, most of whom showed great interest in what we were doing and helped us in any way they could. I guess these first few years of independent living were very formative regarding the future.

Back in the UK I moved quickly on to my next challenge, that had been planned before I left for the overland trip. I took up a course in Youth & Community Work at Westhill College in Birmingham. One of the reasons I had left the Merchant Navy was a desire to 'work with people'. I wasn't quite sure what that meant but there was a gut feeling that this was a direction I should take which was salted with a hefty dose of Christian commitment.

I had been brought up in a fairly well off family in rural Kent. We lived in the middle of a wood near Toys Hill, where my parents had built three houses just after World War 2. Both sets of grand parents lived nearby, as did other members of the family. My Mother's Father was very active in our local village of Brasted and the Anglican Church, where I was christened and confirmed. I went regularly to Church, somewhat reluctantly in my teens before I left for sea but I guess those years had laid a foundation of faith in my life. Whilst engaged in the shore based naval training in Plymouth, however, I realised there was a lot more to Christianity than just going to church and this resulted in a decision to put God at the centre of things. This radically altered the direction of my life and has influenced it ever since. There is probably a book lurking behind this story in itself, but that will have to wait until another day. Suffice to say I became involved with various contemporary expressions of Christianity under such names as the 'charismatic, house church, restoration and renewal movements' which will mean little to anyone outside these rather closed and narrow streams of the faith. To be honest they ended up leaving me out in the cold. I still consider myself a Christian, have faith and believe God holds my destiny in his hand but I have largely withdrawn from organised religion as much of my experience has caused me to question the motives behind it. It seems to have more to do with the abuse of power than caring concern, integrity and maturity in leadership. Neither am I convinced that this situation is limited to the Christian religion alone!

Pinehurst, *the house my parents built and home for my first 16 years. When finished, the house was front page news.*

Pinehurst *as it is today.*

During the course I met and married my wife, Usha, also a Christian but from a Hindu background. On completion of her teacher training we moved to York to take up my first youth work appointment. We had some very happy years in the city and during this time our first two children, Nayna and John, were born. We also met another couple at the church we went to, just starting out on family life; Rob and Therese Ringer became great friends, encouraged by the fact that Rob and I shared a common interest in kayaking, walking and cycling.

We organised various activities with a close circle of friends. The "I went kayaking with Rob and Richard and survived" trips became legendary. Occasionally Rob and I would organise mini-expeditions on our own or with a few friends in support.

Perhaps the most challenging of these were two Trans-Penine Canal Marathons, a 127 mile non stop kayak across the Penines on the Leeds Liverpool Canal, made no easier by strong headwinds, horizontal rain, sleet and ice on the boat!

The Ringers and Woods began taking holidays together, starting a tradition that would last for many years. Whilst on one such Christmas log cabin holiday in Keilder Forest it had snowed heavily and a cycle ride along some of the forest tracks seemed like a good idea. We were on the return leg of the route and the snow had started again. Both Rob and I were looking forward to several drinks around a warm electric fire, but for some reason the Forestry Commission didn't seem to think open log fires were a good idea in their wooden cabins! It was getting dark and a thunderstorm had just begun. This was extremely bizarre, as I had never experienced thunder and lightening in a snowstorm before! As we slipped and slid along the main road before the turning for the cabin, there was a tremendous flash of electric blue light and a huge explosion, fire and sparks erupted from a wooden electric pylon and we realised that we had just witnessed a spectacular lightening strike. I think we pedalled a little faster over the last half mile!

In 1987 we moved to Worcester. 1994 was a major family landmark when our third child, Joshua, was born. With a 10 year gap between him and John, plus the fact of having a baby around, this event pretty much put an end to shared family holidays. Our children were growing up and consequently priorities changed. However, Rob and I still maintained the occasional foray into the wilds, with kayaking taking the back seat to mountain biking, which sometimes proved a painful pursuit. On one occasion, having circumnavigated the Isle of Mull, we were heading for Strontium back on the mainland. I took a sharp bend in driving rain at high speed, not a good combination, and ended up crashing onto a rock-strewn bank. Fortunately I was wearing a helmet otherwise I probably would have suffered severe head injuries if the dent was anything to go by, but the rocks that came into contact with my chest didn't do my ribs any good at all! We were still two days away from the end of the trip and a long way from anywhere so the rest of the journey was rather painful, especially on the steeper hills when the breathing got heavier against the cracked ribs!

It wasn't just these trips and mini-expeditions that helped quench my search for a fuller life. I am the kind of person who has a constant desire to face new and varied challenges, both small and large, and this has been reflected in the work I have done over the years. I have been employed in youth work for more than 20 years, but the major expertise I have gained is in the development and implementation of project based work. This has entailed organising a number of cutting edge initiatives, from the seed of an idea through the funding process, to initiation and completion. I did hold the record for the world's largest cheque on a single sheet of paper, part of the wider work of 'Christmas Cracker' a youth fund raising initiative of which I was Project Director for over six years. During this time, local youth groups took part in a national challenge each Christmas, to raise funds for the Developing World. We organised, 'Eat Less, Pay More' restaurants, live broadcasting on FM radio stations, 'Fair Trade Shops and Newspapers', all of which raised over £4 million. It was a brilliant effort by the thousands of young people and youth workers who were involved, proving what could be achieved with great ideas, the will to succeed and the time and energy of committed individuals on a steep learning curve! I love helping others to realise their potential and achieve things they didn't think they were capable of; youth work provides a great vehicle for facilitating this but remains one of the most misunderstood professions. It has very little to do with table tennis and 'keeping the kids off the streets' and has a great deal to do with enabling young people to make the transition from being a child to adult life in as creative a manner as possible. This is all about the discovery of self, learning how to conduct yourself effectively with others, finding out just what you are capable of and astonishing yourself when you find you are able to realise that capability.

I am not a maintenance person, I get bored easily once the challenge has been achieved or the particular piece of work has lost the pioneering element from it. I am not really interested in pursuing a particular path either, preferring to take hold of a thing and work on it, whilst engaging in the learning process necessary to gain expertise and fulfil the goal. I think I would be very unhappy following a particular career path, for instance, where you continue to do the same thing year upon year, with a view to promotion or more knowledge and expertise in the same area. Don't get me wrong, there is nothing negative about this way of life, in fact there are times when I wish that I could just settle into something more secure and predictable, but I don't think it will ever happen.

Having said that, everyone's life is a challenge, filled with personal mountains to climb or oceans to cross. These can be small and seemingly insignificant to others but may be enormous to the individual concerned, requiring all our energy and strength to tackle. Sometimes we fail, sometimes spectacularly, but living to fight another day, feeling stronger and wiser as a result, is surely what life is all about? I believe life is a gift to both the person it has been given to and those they come into contact with. Our supreme challenge is to use that gift to its full extent both personally and for others. Setting goals and achieving them is part and parcel of the process that also entails learning from the times when we fail. In fact 'process' is a fantastically important part of life, often missed by many. It is something that should be at the heart of most things. As youth workers we are as interested in how an individual reaches an outcome, as in the fact that they actually succeeded in getting there. Perhaps it is the journey, the process of getting there, which fascinates me. In 1997 the process began for the journey of a lifetime.

Chapter Two

Early 1998 saw Rob and I heading for Scotland. The miles steadily slipped by as we pushed northward for another mountain bike trip. Our intention was to base ourselves at Inverary and cycle around the mountains and coastal region of the area. Unbeknown to him, I was armed with a file of the recent Atlantic Rowing Race, information I had systematically collated from the internet over previous months. I enjoyed these excursions of ours but felt the time had come for a more substantial challenge. As the 2001 race required teams of two, Rob was the obvious choice of partner. As well as our long standing family friendship we had both been through many tough, challenging and sometimes dangerous situations which had developed a high level of mutual trust, respect and understanding. Relaxing in some distant pub in front of a log fire with some good food and drink after a hard day on the road helped greatly to cement our friendship, not to mention a developing taste for the finer qualities of single malt whiskey!

I lifted the file from the back seat and handed it to Rob, "Fancy a go at this?" I asked. Rob opened it and began to reading. Apart from the noise of the car I realised that an all pervading silence had settled on our journey. Rob's initial reaction was less than enthusiastic but after a few pints in the pub that evening he seemed to be warming to the idea! We had an enjoyable few days on the road but didn't talk much about the Atlantic Challenge. We returned to Appleby and just before leaving for Worcester I asked him to let me know whether or not he was up for it.

In the meantime I had heard from race organisers, The Challenge Business, that a second event was to be staged in 2001. It would start from Tenerife in October and would be open to 50 crews of two in standard one design boats, which each team would be responsible to purchase and build from its original kit form.

Registration was on a first come first served basis and I was desperate to make sure our entry would arrive at Challenge Business HQ ahead of the rest, securing our place. I rang Rob for a final decision as we had to send completed application forms with photos and an initial cheque for £150 each. Rob confirmed his intention to join the team and, on June 6th, 1998, I posted the payment and paperwork, marking the beginning of the long and all consuming road to the start line.

The thing that struck me about this first major step was the transition from an idea to reality. I experienced a genuine change which I can only describe as one of those significant defining moments in life. Prior to this point the race was something out there that other people had experienced, I could rationalise many reasons why I should not go ahead with it: family, financial commitments, a reasonable job and at 42, it could be argued, that it was not the optimum time in life to try and transcend from a basic level of fitness to that of an endurance athlete! Oh yes, and the small matter of finding the estimated £50,000 in cash and kind needed to complete the enterprise, could have also been a bit of a stumbling block! Someone once asked me, 'are you creative within or subject to your circumstances?' This has been one of those pearls of wisdom which I have often fallen back on when making those big decisions that seem to push back the boundaries of 'normal' life; I guess this was time to be creative!

I received confirmation that we had been successfully registered, so set about researching what would be involved and how we would tackle the major challenges ahead.

I made the decision to try and attract a main national sponsor within the period from June to October 1998. After that we had to start paying ten quarterly instalments to the Challenge Business of £1,150, which would eventually make up the £11,500 race fee the organisers required. This excluded the £300 registration sent with the initial application and £2,350 to cover the cost of the boat kit. The other £11,500 was to cover administration costs and the provision of two Challenge Business Yachts which would act as safety vessels throughout the duration of the race. At least that was our assumption, because despite requesting it, a complete breakdown of this sum never materialised from the organisers.

I had some help to design a logo and letterhead, put together some resource materials and began writing to potential sponsors. I compiled a 'hit list' of companies that a number of people had suggested, representing a broad swathe of different businesses. The reasons for targeting each one were varied. I had been a long term customer of some, others had links with water sports, boating and all things maritime; a few resulted from contacts given to me and the rest had local or regional profile.

I began this process full of hope and enthusiasm, after all fewer people had rowed an ocean successfully than reached the summit of Everest. Surely the visionaries of UK plc would be inspired by our brave quest, emulating the great British tradition of expeditions and adventure!

The replies, however, soon revealed zero inspiration and a total lack of vision. They generated two fairly standard responses which became boringly predictable. Firstly, no response at all, or secondly, a standard letter saying, thanks but our budget is spent for this year, even though we wouldn't have supported you anyway, however we wish you luck. This was a bit depressing, especially as the odds of corporate 'luck' financing our Challenge where even less than those surrounding the purchase of a Lottery ticket! On rare occasions I would receive a personal response from a potential sponsor, albeit negative, but clearly the individual had taken the time to read the letter and consider my request, which was vaguely encouraging. One of these came from Fran Cotton, boss of the clothing company, Cotton Traders. I had been a long time customer of his and thought it worth a shot, but unfortunately it missed the target, even though I still wear the trousers!

Having written hundreds of letters, none of which bore any fruit, it became a little wearing when well intentioned individuals said for the hundredth time, 'why don't you try Richard Branson'! The fact is we did, experiencing the same boringly predictable replies, on both occasions.

At the same time Rob was pursuing one or two contacts to link with national charities. This looked very promising at one point but despite initially positive meetings and telephone conversations, the information never seemed to get so far as the decision makers.

I guess it was worth a shot, but the huge amount of time to execute this relatively expensive exercise for no result represented the first great hurdle to overcome in our bid for success. However if you set yourself the challenge of rowing an ocean, giving up at this stage is not an option: it was time to alter course.

Finance wasn't everything however. I only had limited rowing experience, much of it gained during the training to qualify as a lifeboat coxswain whilst in the Merchant Navy.

To achieve this, all eight Cadets and the Cadet Instruction Officer (CIO) would launch one of the ship's lifeboats from davits situated up to 70 feet above sea level, depending on how heavily laden the MS *Manora* was at the time. We would take it in turns to command this operation, which entailed releasing the boat from its lashings, lowering it over the side to deck level, embarking the rest of the team, controlling its descent to the sea below and then climbing 70 feet down a rope ladder to the waiting boat. Not a task for the faint hearted or anyone suffering from vertigo! Having motored away from the ships side we would then begin the task of rowing round the port, each of us using a big wooden oar to contribute to the propulsion of this great white fibre glass tub, achieving a pace only a snail would have been proud of! Upon conclusion of the rowing exercise, we would return to the ship, 'rest on our oars', 'toss our oars' and stow them. The lifeboat falls would then be attached to the bow and stern, whilst one of us began the long climb back up to the boat deck to operate the winch. It would then be brought back up and secured ready for another exercise or a real emergency at sea. Once we were all proficient at this procedure, we were examined for competency and if successful, awarded our Lifeboat Coxswains certificate, an accolade we all managed to achieve!

That really summed up my experience apart from a few trips of varying length in rowing boats on rivers, lakes and the sea whilst on holidays or days out. Of course I wasn't a stranger to the sea, ships or boats, and had extensive experience of a variety of craft in different situations. Kayaking was the one sport that I had probably engaged in more than any other on a consistent basis. In fact when I was still at school I went on a course in Scotland that ended on a high note, shooting Grand Tully rapids after a 12 mile paddle down the River Tay. I distinctly remember the impending sense of doom as I approached a large rock at the top of the rapid. This could have had something to do with the roar of water as the river disappeared either side of the rock and gave illusion of nothing beyond except space. Being so low in the water you couldn't see beyond what was immediately in front of you, until you were about to be propelled into the churning water of the rapid as it fell away either side of the rock. It was my turn, the rock flashed past as I entered the rapid via the right hand channel, I was catapulted into a maelstrom of water going at a colossal rate. I paddled for all I was worth and, as quickly as it had started, it was all over. I had survived with a wonderful sense of excitement probably fuelled by a combination of adrenaline and terror coursing through my veins. It was great!

I had also got a taste for sea kayaking and decided to build my own craft. I bought a plywood kit and constructed it in a room over my Dad's garage. It performed very well and gave me a great deal of pleasure. The construction of the kayak was also based on the use of fibreglass resin and tape and subsequently I built a Canadian canoe in the same way. Part of the Atlantic Challenge was to build the boat we would compete in, so this experience gave me a bit of expertise and a lot more confidence than I would otherwise have had.

Anyway, I decided in June that I should head for the Worcester Rowing Club and see if I could pick up a few tips and basic rowing skills. The Atlantic boats used sliding seats and the rowing technique is similar to that used by those who delight in propelling a vessel not much wider than a pencil at the fastest speed possible down a river or across a lake. The rowing fraternity are a funny lot; I'm not really sure whether they comprehended the exact nature of my proposal, although one club member did say his son had thought of entering the Atlantic Race but decided pulling the project together, especially from a financial perspective, put him off. I eventually managed to contact the right person to give me some instruction and he offered to put me through their 'Watermanship' course. I thought it would be a good idea for Rob to do this as well but his distant location in Cumbria did cause a slight logistical problem. My coach therefore agreed to give him a crash course, (not sure that was the most motivational thing to call it!) over a couple of weekends later in the year. So on Sunday, June 29th, 1998, I arrived at the Club for my initiation into the art of rowing Redgrave style.

I started off in a fibre glass boat with a relatively broad beam designed for greater stability, presumably to limit the potential for the hapless novice to experience a nervous breakdown by the end of the first session, as your whole concentration centres on trying to stay upright and not much else. Added to this, a length of line was attached to the boat for the first couple of lessons so if you did lose control, and that is a word I use with some caution at this stage of the game, at least the boat could be retrieved whilst you floated off to your inevitable doom over the weir at Diglis! I quickly progressed to being able to row the boat at the same time as sliding the seat back and forth. The idea is to use the power in your legs to give the maximum effect in propelling the boat forwards. Of course one of the major problems, peculiar to rowers, is not being able to see where you are going. Most people in their right minds think it better to look in the direction of travel and thus avoid contact with other craft or objects that may inevitably bring down disaster upon you. Rowers, however, think it better to see where you have been. I guess it has certain advantages when racing, especially if you happen to be in the lead, at least you can keep an eye on the opposition, but the general assumption seems to be that everything gives way to oars, which is fine, until the boat tries to apply this rule to the bank!

I had one or two lessons a week and started to get the hang of things. I progressed to a much sleeker wooden scull, the name given to boats that are driven by a rower with two oars, or blades, as those 'in the know' call them, with an occasional outing in a larger boat with a Cox and second rower. My coach told me that if you can master sculling then rowing won't be a problem. Well, whatever, all I wanted to be able to do was gain some knowledge and technique that would give me enough expertise to haul a tonne of boat 3,000 miles across the Atlantic as efficiently as possible whilst avoiding unnecessary injury. It was rather ironic that the injury I finally sustained had nothing to do with the actual task of rowing.

Later in the summer Rob came down for his rowing course. I think he tried to do it over three days. Anyway, at the weekend we took a double scull out together. Rob was extremely nervous about the stability of the boat, even with all our experience of kayaks it feels like you are starting all over again. We sculled up the river turned and started back towards the Club. As we progressed our confidence grew and with it, the speed of the boat. The Worcester Race Course runs beside the River Severn and the main stand backs on to the river. The stairs leading to the various levels of the stand have glass all the way up on the outside wall that overlooks the river and on that day it was packed with punters going about their sporting business. We were feeling pretty pleased with ourselves as we powered our way past the crowd, when suddenly one of the oars missed a stroke and the next thing we knew, the boat was capsizing and we were unceremoniously dumped in the drink. The water was quite warm and pleasant but the thought of contracting Weils disease and the need to get the boat back to the landing stage became our priority. The embarrassment caused by the obvious amusement of the race going public had nothing to do with the speed at which we completed this task of course!

A few weeks later I completed my 'Watermanship Course' successfully and was awarded a certificate to prove it. I had attained a reasonable level of competency and felt more confident about rowing. I was also starting to get fitter and thereby hangs another tale.

I wouldn't say that I was unfit when we first set out on the Atlantic journey, but I certainly felt I had a long way to go to reach the level of fitness I imagined necessary to survive the ordeal. I didn't really know much about what I needed to do, when I needed to do it and how often. Even if I had been confident about this, I had nowhere to go that had the necessary equipment and support, but help was at hand and this came as a result of a rather unusual encounter.

Rob had been having some work done on his house in Appleby, the builder had left a pile of sand he did not need and so he offered it to a guy who lived up the road. He came round to collect it and during the ensuing conversation Rob told him about the Challenge and our need for support with training. It turned out that Rob's new found acquaintance was a lecturer in high altitude nutrition at University College Chester. He travelled all over the world giving lectures on the subject and suggested that Rob should contact Dave Kellett, the Head of the Sports Science Department in Chester. As a result of this introduction we were invited to a meeting with Dave and a group from the Department to discuss the possibilities of a link with them. The meeting took place in November 1998 and it was agreed that a group of staff and students from the Department would look at all aspects of training up to and including the race itself. Their support would cover physiological, psychological and nutritional input, with the development of a weekly training programme. We would also be asked to come to Chester for testing every couple of months and occasionally conduct a 24-hour row in the lab and one 48-hour row. They wanted to do a Phd study on us that would be published after the race and part of the reason for these extended rows were to collect data under laboratory conditions. We arranged a date for our first testing session and headed home.

At about the same time my nearest Health Club in Worcester had been taken over by the national Cannons chain. Paul Weighton had recently become Manager and I approached him to ask if he would be willing to give me a complementary membership in return for a logo on the boat and other PR opportunities. He was very supportive and enthusiastically agreed to give his full support, along with his staff and club facilities. It was the first real breakthrough with regard to a tangible offer of genuine support and I left the meeting not only very grateful but extremely happy that at last I had something to show for all those hours spent writing letters and making phone calls, otherwise to no avail. It was also a real landmark in my strategy for support and sponsorship.

Chapter Three

I had decided back in June, that if the national strategy proved unsuccessful I would abandon this and target my efforts on a regional basis. The first stage payment to the Challenge Business was also imminent, which added to the urgency of gaining some success with sponsorship. I recognised that there was real potential to use the Challenge as a major fund raising and awareness project; if I could forge links with a local charity it would also enable me to put something back into the community. So I picked up the phone and made a call to the local Hospice.

I spoke to Mary Jenks, an old friend and Volunteer Co-ordinator for St Richard's Hospice. I told Mary what I was up to, asking whether the Hospice would be interested in teaming up with us. She was very positive and suggested that I contact Angela Hughes, who was in charge of fund raising. I called her and said, "You will probably think I am mad and this phone call may be as far as this proposal goes, but I am planning to row the Atlantic in a couple of years and wondered if you might be interested in using the project to benefit the Hospice". She was equally as enthusiastic as Mary but said she would have to talk to various people and let me know. These positive responses appeared too good to be true, first Chester Sports Scientists, then Cannons and now the Hospice. Making the project something the local community in South Worcestershire could be involved in seemed to be the right decision after all the setbacks of pursuing an unrewarding national strategy. Whether or not this would prove to be the case longer term, only time would tell, but for now it was nice to experience some positive feedback at last!

After a short interval Angela was in touch again, inviting both Rob and I to a meeting with various Hospice staff and volunteers. After a warm greeting we presented the project to the assembled company and were plied with questions on all aspects of the Challenge. We discussed what the Hospice might be able to get from the process and made it clear that we wanted to keep the money raised for the building and equipping of the boat separate from funds dedicated to the Hospice. The Executive Director of St Richard's Hospice, Barney Price, chaired the meeting; he not only ended up as one of the key players in making the project a success but also became a good friend.

The decision was made to link the project with St Richard's, subject to an independent assessment as to it's 'value' which would be conducted by an outside consultant on behalf of the Governors. This was completed over the following weeks and came out in our favour. As a result the Governors gave the go ahead and then Barney told us we had received an anonymous gift of £5,000 from a 'well wisher' linked with the Hospice. This was fantastic news as it meant that we were able to pay the first instalment of £1,150, and order the boat kit so we could start work on the build.

Whilst all this was going on I was beginning to give some attention to contacting various people within the Worcester business community. Throughout my time in Worcester I had been a customer of a local business called Athena. They made signs, banners and branded clothing. In my capacity as a youth worker we were often doing events and projects that required publicity and promotion, and I had got to know the owner of the business, Richard Lovell, quite well. I thought he might be interested in helping with the project so I approached him for support. His response was overwhelmingly positive. We discussed the challenge and various ideas for raising sponsorship. The main one was to organise a 'West Midlands Rowing Challenge', the idea being to recruit individuals in schools, health clubs, businesses and various organisations, to set up teams of 24 and do a sponsored row on Concept 2 rowing machines throughout November 1999. We took the idea to a meeting at the Hospice with estimates as to how much it was likely to realise, and the terms Richard was willing to operate under. Basically, the agreement was to give a percentage of the money raised to sponsor the boat and crew and split the rest between the Hospice and Richard, in order to cover his costs whilst supporting the overall work of the Hospice. His offer was extremely generous because he undertook to fund the whole enterprise through his business and if it failed to achieve what we thought it could, he was willing to underwrite the cost. I think his willingness was indicative of two things, firstly his great confidence in the overall success of the project and secondly his courage to take a risk and support a project he obviously believed in. Richard became an integral part of our preparations for the challenge throughout 1999 and the early part of 2000, and it was partly due to his vision and enthusiasm that we progressed as far and as fast with our preparations in the initial stages.

1998 was about to be consigned to the annals of history, but just before Christmas I sent the second stage payment to the Challenge Business in advance of the 1st January deadline. I also included the £2,350 payment for the boat kit. We had decided to build the boat ourselves rather than use the option of a professional builder. We knew we could save a considerable amount of money by following this course of action; Rob and I also thought this was in the spirit of the challenge and felt that we would miss out on a whole area of experience if we handed the construction over to someone who didn't really own the project.

1999 dawned and on January 10th the first gathering of registered teams took place at Baden Powell House in London. Rob and I decided to pay our first visit to the London Boat Show the day before and then go on to the meeting the next day. I don't recall how many teams were signed up at that stage but there was a good turn out with representatives from all over the world. The meeting itself was quite informative and interesting, with items including training, fitness, weather and medical input from some of the competitors in the 97/98 race. We met Chay Blyth, the boss of the Challenge Business for the first time, who introduced the challenge in the off-handed manner that became a characteristic of his input over the next couple of years. He introduced the race in the context of "just a bit of fun"; with hindsight the ensuing laughter was somewhat naive, particularly as the outcome of the Challenge Business's 'organisation' of the project turned out to be less than amusing!

Outside the venue, 'This Way Up' had been parked; it was interesting to see an Atlantic rowing boat for the first time. Ironically this one had retired in the early stages of the first race in 1997. Rob and I were inspired to get the kit and start the construction of our boat as soon as possible.

On January 31st we went to University College Chester for the first of our fitness assessments. We met various people who would be helping us over the next couple of years. At this stage the two main people involved were James Ryder and Gareth Jones. They were both with us throughout the whole period, with various others dipping in and out of the team as time went on. Gareth's main responsibility was physiology and he put together the training programmes whilst James was primarily responsible for nutrition. These training assessments were really hard and never became any easier, particularly the VO2 max tests that calculate the amount of oxygen your muscles can absorb and thus give a measure of fitness. The fitter you are the better your muscles absorb oxygen and the more efficient you become. The problem with the testing is the way you have to increase the effort you put in to a particular exercise until you can go no further because of exhaustion. In these early days we did this by running on a treadmill. The speed did not vary but every couple of minutes the incline on the machine was increased. After about 10-12 minutes of this, the 'Grim Reaper' would enter the lab and you knew it was time to stop before he got too close. After the first few bi-monthly visits the treadmill was replaced by a rowing machine. This was a great relief as I really don't like running and doing the thing you were training for was much more specific and far more accurate. It also gave an indication of progress. Following this initial visit our first training programme came through and the quest for fitness began. We were given specific plans tailored for our own needs, which were a combination of aerobic work, resistance training with weights, stretching, core stability, and hours and hours on the rowing machine doing a variety of different exercises partly to make things vaguely interesting. The training was quite tough but not impossibly so. I rose to the challenge and in the main enjoyed the experience throughout, even having to be at the gym for 0630 hours up to six days a week in the closing stages (so I had time to get through it all and carry on with the day job). It made me realise just how fortunate professional sports people are, given the chance to train all day and get paid into the bargain, especially those whose annual income is probably greater than the GNP of a small Third World Country!

On Saturday, 27th February, 1999, I had a meeting with Brian Saunders at the Worcester Racecourse Grandstand. Brian was the organiser of the Inland Waterways Festival to be held later in the year. The racecourse is located on an area called Pitchcroft, adjacent to the River Severn, both of which be used as the Festival venue. The Festival is the annual event of the Inland Waterways Association, staged in different parts of the country, and brings together inland water enthusiasts, commercial enterprises, exhibitions and a full programme of events. I realised this would be a brilliant opportunity to launch and officially name our boat, even though, at this stage, the boat kit was not yet available!

Brian was extremely helpful and supportive of my proposal to make the boat and our entry in the race a central feature of the Festival. For the IWA it gave local interest to this national event and it also offered the chance of Sir Chay Blyth coming up to name the boat, as well as officially opening the Festival if he was

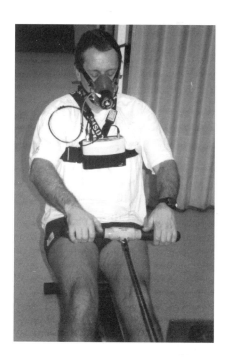

Rob suffering a VO2 max test.

willing to accept my invitation. Over the next few months I had several meetings with Brian and cannot underestimate the value of his help and the kindness with which he gave it. He had a huge job getting this massive event organised and operating smoothly, but every time we met he always had time to listen to my requests and do everything he could to accommodate us. It is this kind of response and working relationship that was to be repeated on many occasions, and I found this one of the most rewarding aspects of the whole project.

The next day Rob and I joined a team of blokes at Cannons Health Club who had organised a 100,000-meter row. There was also a mixed team of five men and five women who would be attempting the challenge with us. We had two Concept II rowing machines set up in the lounge area of the club and thought it would take us about 6 hours to complete. We each did 500 meter 'shifts' before changing over to the next team member as quickly as possible, keeping the machines moving all the time. The row was also dedicated to the Hospice as a fund raising exercise (no pun intended!) and by the end of the day there were 20 very tired team members with very high morale. Ultimately the mixed team slashed 20 minutes off the British record for dry land endurance rowing in a time of six hours 24 minutes and 46 seconds. So far as I recall we completed the 100,000 meters about 10 minutes before the mixed team finished, which I reckon was pretty good going considering our average age. Suffice to say this rate would not reflect our progress across the 'Pond' in a couple of year's time!

Whilst all this was going on news had come through that the boat kit would soon be ready. Rob had gained permission to build the boat in a corner of the Appleby Heritage Centre, just up the road from his house. This excellent venue used to be an old engine shed next to the Seattle-Carlisle line but in recent years had been converted into a training centre. It was mainly used to renovate old railway rolling stock for the many heritage steam railways around the country. This was an enormous boost for the project, as not only did it provide an excellent space for the boat construction but also access to the tools and equipment we would need for the job. It was all provided free of charge and made a great contribution to the project that was gratefully received.

Rob had acquired a rather large trailer from a guy who owned a castle and lived near Appleby. That is totally irrelevant to the story but hey, is it every day you come into contact with a castle owner? Anyway, the trailer would provide the means to collect our long awaited boat kit from Laser Profiles in Poole, Dorset. Our boat was in a batch of five, the rest of which were being shipped overseas, these being the first new design Atlantic boats. One of them was going out to the USA where Tom Mailhot of the American Star team had a boat builder lined up to start construction, more of which later.

We had previously towed the trailer to Worcester and early on Monday, March 15th, I hitched it to the back of my faithful old Cavalier and headed south. This marked the first stage of two and-a-half years of towing abuse accompanied by the occasional heady smell of burning rubber! Suffice to say my trusty old Vauxhall keeps on going after all this and nearly 120,000 miles on the clock, a bit like me really! (Hey Vauxhall! Why not sponsor my next trip!!!) Overkill, would best describe the relative size of the trailer, probably more at home on a farm, but the big question in my mind was how did the designer achieve such an interesting ride? You may remember the old dog food advert.... "There's more dog taste to the ounce in bounce, the tasty, meaty dog food...BOUNCE", I think this held the answer, as it must have been constructed of old Bounce tins!

I eventually arrived at Laser Profiles. It was a fascinating place with large flat cutting tables where the wood or metal would be laid out and many computer controlled lasers cut the material to shape. There in the middle of the loading bay was a stack of five Atlantic rowing boat kits, four bound for overseas and one for us: the first UK team to get their hands on one and eventually the first to finish construction, something we are still proud of achieving. The forklift loaded up the kit and after securing and covering it I began the long trip back to Worcester. Rob met me there, hitched 'El Bounceo' to his car and did the next 200 miles to Appleby where he had arranged a fork lift to unload the kit ready to start the next major stage of the project: boat building!

Our boat kit arrives at Appleby!

Chapter Four

This chapter is all about building the boat, it was a major undertaking and hugely satisfying once completed, in fact I still look at 'her' sometimes and find it hard to believe that she was fashioned with our own hands. I had some experience of boat construction when I built a marine ply sea kayak and Canadian canoe some years ago, but an Atlantic boat, however, is much more of a challenge! Nevertheless both Rob and I felt it was a key part of the overall Atlantic Rowing project, and so we set about the task with enthusiasm.

27 6 feet x 8 feet sheets of 6 & 9 mm marine plywood lay on a pallet on the floor of the Appleby Heritage Centre. Each sheet had individual parts of the boat cut into it with just a few tabs left to hold them to the main sheet. Each piece had a part number marked on it and these corresponded, in theory, to a step by step manual showing you how to build the boat in a pictorial format. There were no written instructions, which made it a bit confusing at times. No one had ever built one of these before, as the original design had been amended for the new race. We had a call from the Challenge Business asking us if we would be prepared to do a comprehensive check list to make sure all the parts were there, and then keep a record of the build with a diary and photographs; this we gladly agreed to.

I was familiar with the use of epoxy resin and glass tape, but an Atlantic boat requires filleting and all sorts of other resin compounds to finish the job. So I turned to the internet and found *www.wessex-resins.com* that has an online manual, which is of great help if you choose to use their products. A little more research under 'epoxy resin' on the search engine brought up more useful information. We decided to 'wet out' the ply with a coat of resin to seal it before construction work began, this greatly prolonging the life of the boat. We also decided not to sheath the hull, i.e. cover the exterior of the hull with a fine layer of glass cloth and resin for extra strength. This didn't seem to give any great advantage and would only add to the weight. Lets face it, if we went hacking down a wave and hit an obstacle like a floating container or tree trunk the result would probably be the same whether or not the hull had been sheathed!

Rob cut all the pieces out of the main sheets and made an inventory. At first we weren't sure all the parts were there but after several phone calls and discussions with the Challenge Business we thought the kit was complete. The Inland Waterways Festival due to take place at the end of August had set our deadline for completion of the boat to basic level. Rob had said the Challenge Business would lend us the old prototype boat if we failed to achieve this, but I said to Rob that as far as I was concerned there was no prototype and the deadline must be achieved. This gave us about five months to complete the task.

Rob did a great deal of preparatory work before I arrived for the first building weekend about mid April. The initial task was to 'wet out' all the parts and we found that the best and probably only efficient way of doing this was to use foam rollers. These would have to be disposed of at regular intervals but any other roller product would leave a residue on the wood (a fact we learnt by experience). Application with brushes took too long and the coat would be too thick, not to mention the brush bill as the resin 'went off' pretty quickly, rendering the brush useless. Once the resin had set we then had to sand it all down and start assembling the pieces. This is quite satisfying as it is a relatively simple task that happens quickly, so you feel you are progressing reasonably fast. The construction is what they call 'self-jigging', which means the hull takes shape as you pull the parts together and hammer in pegs that secure the pieces in a dry form ready for filleting to begin.

Quite a lot happened throughout the period April to August apart from the boat building but don't worry, as I will catch up on all that in the next chapter. However the dominant feature of our preparations remained the pile of ply, gallons of epoxy and loads of other seemingly endless noxious substances amassing like some deadly army prior to advancing on its foe....in this case us! We soon realised that if the fumes or liquids didn't get us, then the over heating epoxy might blow us up, or perhaps we would be entombed in it should we not apply it fast enough. Anyway it was reassuring to know that if none of this happened then the dust from endless sanding to finish the job would probably deliver the coup de grace to one or other of us! I suspect if we had been tested for illegal substances at this point in our preparations the results would have left the boffins extremely baffled!

Anyway enough of this! It's amazing how you get bits of advice along the way that are really helpful (not withstanding the fact that you get an awful lot that isn't as well!) and one such gem came from someone who suggested the best way to fillet the joints once the dry assembly of the boat was done was to use plastic cake icing bags. So off I went to my local cake accessory shop in Worcester and asked if they had such things.

"Yes" replied the shop assistant "How many do you want?"
"How many in a box?" I replied.
"100" she said.
"I'll have a box full then please!"
She looked a little perplexed, it was written all over her face, 'what was this guy doing, setting up a cake icing factory, could he be the first male member of the Women's Institute?' I thought I should put her out of her misery and told her I was rowing the Atlantic in a couple of years, needed a boat for the task which we were in the process of building and these bags would help to join all the bits of wood together! At this point she was looking even more confused! Was this nutter going to row the Atlantic in a wooden boat held together by some inexplicable means with 100 cake icing bags? I thought I'd better quit while I was ahead and left the shop having ordered a box for 50 quid. As it happened this proved to be one of the best bits of boat building advice we gained and I would highly recommend the use of plastic icing bags to make a very ship shape job of filleting resin joints.

In case you aren't sure what filleting joints actually means, imagine you have two pieces of plywood at right angles to each other forming a joint, you mix up your normal resin compound and hardener, and then mix in some filleting compound, (a very light weight powder that thickens and stiffens the resin) and this is 'injected' along the right angle to form a joint. Once complete and before it sets you run a wooden spatula over the compound to tidy it up and for a really strong finish a layer or two of fibreglass tape and resin is added at a later date. No nails or screws are used, the whole boat is eventually held together by this means and once formed becomes incredibly strong.

I ended up doing the 400 mile round trip to Cumbria more or less every other weekend. In the meantime Rob recruited some help from one or two local people including a work colleague called Al, who became a key part of this phase. It was always an encouragement to come up and find that work had progressed in my absence; ultimately the boat building became Rob's major contribution to the whole project and it is worth noting that he made an excellent job of it.

The first stages of the build were executed with an inverted hull. It was important to get this right before turning the boat over, upright, otherwise you end up making the job 10 times more difficult by working underneath and thereby not having the help of gravity to fill the joints with the resin. Not only that but working with sanding equipment when the hull is overhead is very taxing physically.

Applying resin to the inverted hull.

Whilst we were in full production in Cumbria, one of the other five kits that had been waiting for collection when I went to Laser Profiles had been shipped out to the USA. Tom had ordered it for his American bid in the Challenge. Apparently he had lined up a professional boat builder to construct his craft a move that he would live to regret. By the time we had launched our boat he had ended up with a banana shaped hull that ultimately had to be scrapped. I was devastated when I heard this news, as there is a real camaraderie that builds between teams who are sharing experiences that require huge amounts of time and dedication. When another team suffers such a set back you can only empathise and offer any help you can. In the end Tom had to purchase a second kit that he built himself. We saw the end result in Tenerife, which was fabulous, and a real credit to his dedication. I guess the moral is to do it yourself if you want it doing properly. Having said that many other teams had their boats professionally built but in my opinion they missed out on a major part of the challenge and a great deal of satisfaction in putting together the means by which your dream will ultimately succeed or fail.

Before turning the hull over we fitted the transom. We later discovered this was back to front, which wasn't a major problem but happened as a result of unclear instructions in the build manual and probably lost us about half a days work as we deliberated on why the holes for the cabin top didn't locate properly once we got to that stage. Fortunately all it ultimately meant was that these holes had to be made about half an inch wider and then filled.

The major change in design from the 1997 boats was the addition of about four inches of keel running along the whole length of the hull and becoming much deeper at the stern. This became a hot issue for debate amongst competitors as to whether or not it was really necessary, particularly those who bought the old design boats which did not have a keel the full length of the boat. In early conversations Teresa

Rob & the author (left) working on the aft cabin and troublesome transom.

Evans at the Challenge Business had told me the original design boats would not be allowed in the 2001 race, but there was obviously a change in policy along the way. This wasn't a problem for us as we always intended building our own boat but it did mean a keel had to be added to this old design to comply with race rules. The whole keel issue became even more bizarre when teams with new boat kits cut the keel off, although in one case a boat builder recommended to the team by the organisers did this. In the end all boats had to have keels and there was a great deal of last minute panic amongst some to comply. Having said all that it was never an issue for us, the build document was clear, as were the rules.

It was a day for celebration when we turned the hull. Prior to this we taped all the exterior hull joints and sanded everything down. In retrospect we should have finished these with finishing compound and got the upturned hull to a point where all we needed to do was start the paint job, but this is a policy that emerged from hindsight and just made our lives a bit more difficult when we started the paint job. If you do ever decide to build one of these boats however, start with the hull inverted and do as much work on finishing the hull as possible before turning it over. Do not start the paint job in advance, though, as it will get dirty and damaged and you will have problems with joints if the paint gets near the epoxy and does not make contact with the wood.

Now the hull was chocked up on trestles, the right way up we began to feel a real sense of progression. We began work on the interior compartments, cabin, gunwales and deck. The side panels, particularly at the bow were very hard to put on with a great deal of work being necessary to clamp them into place before sealing and taping the joints.

Left: Work started on the cabin interior once the hull was turned.

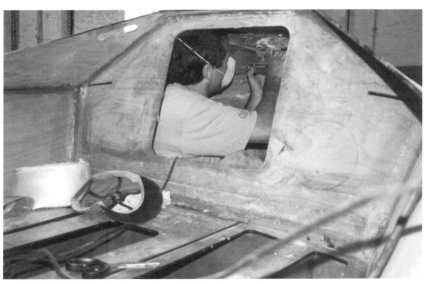

Rob in the bow cabin with a sander, a nasty job!

As we progressed many questions about the build were raised that needed answers. The opportunity to ask people with experience was limited because there weren't that many around nor did I have any knowledge of the Ocean Rowing Society at this time, who ultimately have all the contacts, expertise and more importantly are willing to share it. In fact as we finished being the first of the new design boat builders to complete the task, we ended up offering a good deal of advice to others from our experience. Incidentally as a result of being first to build a new boat, we were 'awarded' race number two. The Kiwi Team who won the first race retained number one. There were many rumours surrounding the race, one I picked up was that the Kiwi Team, which had entered two boats in the race, were after number two as well as one, quite amusing if this was true but it was probably only one of the many myths surrounding the race. If it wasn't, at least we beat the Kiwi's with the boat building. The only problem with that achievement is it wasn't a race in the first place! However, perhaps this is just part of the eccentricity of being British and why we are so successful as a nation! Who knows….in fact who cares?!

We made many decisions about how to do certain things and most of them proved wise, although we would make a number of changes in the light of experience, more of which later. One thing we did decide from day one was that strength and safety were key to our entry. If that meant adding a little more weight we would do so. I had been in seas up to Force 10 with 60-foot waves and I wasn't about to compromise safety for the sake of a few faster miles. There will always be a great deal of debate about this area. The accepted view is, the lighter the boat the faster it will go. I am sure that many corners could be cut to save a few pounds or even ounces here and there and if unlimited funds were available you could name your boat 'As Light as a Feather'. You hear all these strange stories of people in sea going yacht races who are only allowed to take half a toothbrush to save on weight! Surely having your teeth decay on one side of your mouth will ultimately be far more of a problem than the tiny extra weight of a whole toothbrush! Basically, as long as there are competitive people out there with races to be won and records to be broken, people will compromise safety and cut corners. Let's face it, we see it all the time in industry, stay out a bit longer, don't renew that vital piece of gear etc. In the end someone has to carry the can of responsibility and in the case of Ocean Rowing I guess this lies with the competitor… but does it? As I am digressing from the boat building theme of this chapter into health and safety issues I will re visit this later, but I do think this is a subject for further debate.

Building a boat is one thing, doing it on a limited budget is another! During the bits in between all this activity in Cumbria I continued to try and raise sponsorship either in cash or kind to keep the show on the road. In the end, potential supporters were far more willing to give in kind rather than cash. I contacted the Chairman of Sealine International in the early days; Sealine builds luxury cabin cruisers in Kidderminster, about 12 miles from Worcester. He was very helpful and provided all the building materials plus two hand-held GPS units. Another sponsorship story centred round International Coatings, the major paint manufacturer. Rob had written to them regarding sponsorship in kind and had received the all too familiar 'thanks but no thanks' reply. I had then been in touch via a Challenge Business contact Teresa had given me. I was put in touch with the regional sales person and we had lunch at Cannons Health Club where I was training. We struck a deal where he would have a presence on our stand at the Inland Waterways Festival later in the year and International Coatings would supply all our paint needs and advice. This was really fantastic especially with the personal touch that happened when the regional rep for Rob's area came along with the anti fouling paint and helped us apply it. The 'deal' included primer, undercoats, high quality resin based top coat, gloss for the cabin interior, bilge paint, non slip deck paint and anti fouling. During the building we had all the resources provided by the Appleby Heritage Centre at our disposal, which was also a great help as without it we would have had to invest heavily in tools and other accessories to do the job. There was also quite a bit of

The author spent many hours applying products kindly donated by International Coatings.

local interest which included one company that cut stainless steel to our specification in order to mount the rowing gates.

One problem arising was the need to get extra materials to the centre when we wanted to use them. Particularly from my perspective, I didn't want to travel 200 miles and find we could not continue due to lack of the appropriate product being available. I came across a company called Marine Industrial Sealants based near Norwich, which had all the products we needed at reasonable prices and could be ordered over the phone by credit card. They were always very helpful, advising me on the right product for the job and ensuring it would be delivered within a couple of days to Cumbria. I notice the instruction from one of the invoices I have just looked at states, "Leave in coal shed if no one in"; how's that for personal service?

One notable noxious substance was expanding foam. We had decided to fill various compartments with foam. Some of these were too small for practical stowage purposes and others, like the void under the deck in the bow compartment, were to be sealed and without the addition of foam would only be full of air. Having spoken to one team from the 1997 race, who ended up with a hole in the hull and compartments full of water, I concluded that if we hit an underwater obstacle that penetrated the hull, the compartment would lose its buoyancy and we would be rowing with a great deal of extra water ballast to haul along. Because it was sealed it would be very hard to get to and effect a repair. The obvious solution would be to fill key compartments with expanding foam. If the hull was holed the buoyancy would remain intact, and if a catastrophic disaster befell us then at least the boat should remain unsinkable (just like the *Titanic*!). The foam-filling job was my baby and I loved it! The product arrived in two metal cans and you were instructed to mix equal amounts of the thick brown liquids they contained. You then mixed them quickly (10 seconds max) and as you did so, it turned a creamy light brown colour. You then poured it into the space you wished to fill and stood back. The ensuing chemical reaction causes the liquid to expand and turn solid ending up as a block of creamy yellow foam that fills every space. I was told that the reaction was violent enough to bend steel if you didn't allow an escape route until the reaction was complete! Once it had gone off it could be cut to shape with a knife or saw before the deck was laid over it. I guess this gave me some satisfaction because it reminded me of the days of my youth when I used to take great delight in bomb making activities! Now before the Flying Squad comes knocking on my door, there was no malice intended. In those halcyon days they didn't put flame retardant into weed killer powder; if it was mixed with sugar and packed into an empty drinks can with a length of Jetex fuse (as used in model planes to ignite small rocket motors) inserted in the top, you ended up with a fairly lethal item. If this was jammed into an earth bank and the fuse lit, provided you could run reasonably fast, you were unlikely to be blown to smithereens! Once the smoke had cleared you usually found a flat tin and a big hole. Who needs to be an ex Marine, Para, SAS or the like to be an ocean rower?! I'm just ex miss spent youth, ordinary guy!

And then there were the hatches! The build document was very precise: Lewmar Ocean 30, 40 & 60 hatches were to be fitted into the pre cut holes in the bow and cabin. No problem, we bought them with some sponsorship funds, fitted and sealed them…. lovely job! A debate broke out some time later because some of the old boats had Ocean 70s in the cabin and …shock horror they opened upwards, not sideways giving an alleged advantage because of the extra area presented to the wind. I was asked what I felt about this, I guess I was fairly phlegmatic, the rules were clear, obviously some people hadn't left time to alter their boats to comply and I think there may have been one or two fitted despite the rules. In the end the Challenge Business compromised the original rule and said Ocean 70s could be used if they were hinged from the side as opposed to above so no advantage would be given. I think under the circumstances this was a fair decision on the part of the CB but there were still boats with Ocean 70s or equivalent opening upwards at the start. Perhaps it didn't really matter and in this case the advantage gained was probably minimal but race rules are there to create a level playing field and ensure safety for competitors, so the above creates an unnecessary dilemma for race organisers and could ultimately put others at risk…here I go again on the old health and safety band wagon. More later, I promise!

We were cracking on apace, the hull was almost complete and we had come up with some ideas for rowing gear and hatch covers, none of which were covered in the build manual. With completion drawing near we needed to order a trailer. I contacted RM Trailers and had some discussions over the phone. It would not be appropriate to have the same kind of trailer built for the 1997 boats because of the keel problem. The old boats could sit happily on rollers along the base of the hull but with the new design about four inches of nine mm plywood protruded from the base of the hull, and it would have been a good move to have rested the weight of the boat on this. I was also aware that there were key points along the hull where the internal design meant extra strength and the best policy would be to position the rollers on either side at these strongpoints. So I proceeded to draw up diagrams with measurements and sent them to RM to build the trailer accordingly. They did a very good job of this and the result served us very well. It meant you could launch the boat and retrieve her single handed if necessary, although it was a lot easier if there were two of you especially in adverse conditions.

Chapter Five

Whilst the boat gradually took shape up north, the endless tasks of fund raising and training continued. The main emphasis was preparing for the West Midlands Rowing Challenge with Richard Lovell and putting a great deal of time into getting everything into place for launch day at the Inland Waterways Festival. Richard had come up with the idea of building a stand, which would be branded with all the promotional materials he had produced. These included T-shirts, umbrellas, tea towels, clocks and baseball caps. My employers, the Worcestershire Youth Service, had a mobile unit that was loaned for the event. This had its own generator, a lounge and kitchen area for preparation of refreshments. We were going to serve these on the stand at bargain prices to attract the public, the boat providing the centrepiece. We also had a couple of rowing machines for those determined to prove a point by entering a competition we had organised for a bottle of champagne, generating funds for St Richard's Hospice. The Festival organisers had located us right beside the show's main entrance, a prime spot and absolutely brilliant from our perspective: everyone visiting the Festival would have to walk right by our stand.

The boat was now at Richard's business unit for placing various sponsors' logos on the hull and cabin, plus the boat name and those of the crew. Prior to this I had managed to gain the help of another Richard, Richard Underwood, who owned the main builders merchants in Worcester. He provided all the materials for the stand, constructed of large sheets of plywood, which 'Richard L' and his team had painted in the same colours as our boat and covered in text, thanking the various contributors to the project and giving more information about our challenge and the WM Rowing Challenge, which we were hoping many people would sign up for.

Thursday August 25th dawned grey and wet. A colleagues was bringing the mobile unit over from Evesham, which we needed to get into position before stand construction could start. I had been in touch with a contact at Worcester City Council, asking if they would be willing to provide a lorry and driver to pick up the pieces of our stand from Blackpole, transporting them down to Pitchcroft ready for assembly. All of this fell into place at the allotted times and Richard L's crew turned up in force to begin construction. The weather didn't help, though, as Pitchcroft (the site of the Worcester Racecourse adjacent to the River Severn) was gradually being churned up into a veritable quagmire. This didn't look good for the opening of the Festival in 48 hours time!

Undaunted we managed to build the stand and spent Friday sorting out the rest of the bits and pieces we needed to attract the public and put on a really good show. Saturday dawned: it was a beautiful day. In fact the weather was kind to us for the whole weekend, with hot sunshine and blue skies…. perfect! Rob and his family had come down for the occasion and everything looked set for a really good event.

Our stand, at the main entrance of the Inland Waterway Festival, Worcester.

Some weeks earlier I had asked Sir Chay Blyth, boss of the CB, if he would come and name the boat for us. The Inland Waterways Association had asked me if I would also invite him to officially open the Festival just before our ceremony. I wasn't sure what his response would be as he had previously declined to be on a Council of Reference I had been putting together. This was designed to be a body of influential people who had been involved in one way or another with the project and would appear on our letterheads in order to give a kind of 'official stamp' to our entry and thus assist with the quest for sponsorship. Many of them had agreed to give a reference if required to potential supporters. The reason for Sir Chay's reticence was his active involvement in fox hunting! I can almost see the puzzled look on your face at this point so let me explain. Apparently, Sir Chay was regularly engaged in hunting. I had previously invited our local MP to join the Council, which he gladly agreed to. Who, you may well ask, is the MP for Worcester? The answer: Michael Foster, who in 1999 was engaged in his national campaign through his Private Members Bill to ban hunting with dogs! Ooops! I'm still not quite sure why Sir Chay didn't feel able to join the Council of Reference as it had absolutely nothing to do with fox hunting in any way shape or form. Actually Michael is a very nice guy and does a great job for the local community.

Anyway, Sir Chay was kind enough to give a positive response to this latest invitation and we welcomed him on the Saturday along with his wife and Teresa Evans, the race Project Manager who came up from Plymouth with a two pairs of oars!

The actual launch was a logistical nightmare. The boat had never been in the water and, whilst Rob and I had every confidence that she would float, I guess there was always that slight apprehension we might end up as submariners! That aside, Worcester only has one slipway, which, as luck would have it, is a short distance down the road from where I live. It lies at the back of the Sea Scout hut and I had been in touch with them to request permission to launch from there. They were very helpful and gave their consent ,but it is quite steep and has an awkward bend at the top, quite hard to negotiate with a seven metre boat on an eight metre trailer with a range Rover in front! It also lies at least a mile up river from the site of the Festival. We arranged for Richard L to tow the boat from his unit to the river earlier that morning, we successfully negotiated the slipway and our pride and joy slipped easily into the river, floating perfectly! Our finances did not stretch at that point to purchasing a means of propulsion and so I had borrowed two pairs of oars from Jan Meek who had rowed in the 1997 race with her son Dan. I had got to know Jan a little and had been to a presentation she and Dan made in Chipping Campden, where she was formerly the Mayor. Her boat had been virtually abandoned on the Thames and I had been down to pick up the oars on loan some weeks before. The only problem was their respective lengths; one set was about 11 feet long and the other considerably less. Jan had sworn by these shorter oars whilst at sea ,as she found them much easier to handle. I think we found them a bit short and a real miss match if you tried to use them together. As a contingency we had asked Teresa to bring the two pairs they had in Plymouth and so we did our very first row with Jan's oars hoping that Teresa would arrive in time for the official launch!

I must now digress a little, to address the question of oars at this point. Jan's were approximately 10 feet long, her other set were about 11 feet, whilst at the Great River Race in London I had a conversation with a rowers from the 1997 race, who said he thought you should use oars as long as possible. In recent correspondence on the ORS website, Jim Shekhdar, who rowed in the 1997 race and then did the Pacific solo, said: -

On the Atlantic, David and I used 16ft oars and we took 12.5ft oars for rough weather - we didn't use the short ones. On the Pacific I took two pairs of 16ft oars, using the spares as hand rails until one broke, which I then used as the basis for a harpoon to fend off the large shark that took a fancy to my boat.

He seemed to be happy using the extra long pair. I went for length, therefore, and had three pairs from Suttons, all at their maximum length, which is about 11.5 feet. I think the Kiwi teams in the 2001 race used Croker Oars, which are probably lighter than Suttons, but I am not sure about the length. Our oars performed as well as my experience dictates but I cannot really speak with any authority on this subject as I have only used the one type and at one length. I think there is a theory that in heavy weather shorter oars are best, but I am not sure that Jim would agree with this and guess that overall length is relative.

Sir Chay Blyth with Rob and the author, shortly after the boat's launch in 1999.

The author with his proud family, after the launch; from left: Joshua, Usha, John, Nayna & Richard Wood.

Meanwhile back on the River Severn, Rob and I rowed with the mismatched pair, and were both surprised and gratified at the speed and manoeuvrability of our brand new craft. It has to be said that the boat had no equipment, fittings or ballast at this point so it was as light as it ever would be, but suffice to say that we were impressed. We moored the boat under a blue plastic sheet on the opposite bank from Worcester Rowing Club, which marked the site of the impending launch, and left her to carry on with our preparations. Sir Chay duly arrived and so did Teresa with minutes to spare. He officially opened the Festival from Sabrina Bridge, the footbridge over the Severn just below the Club and then made his way around to us. We had brought the boat over the river and unveiled her and after a short introduction from yours truly, Sir Chay sprayed a bottle of champagne over the boat and named her 'The Spirit of Worcestershire' in front of a crowd of about 2,000 people. Rob and I, with Sir Chay aboard, then pulled away from the bank for photos and after dropping him off we rowed down river, turned and came back up to rapturous applause from the crowd and our supporters. It really was a very good event. Earlier in the morning we had done a piece on the river for the regional TV news in addition to stuff for local radio and press. So we also managed to get good media coverage into the bargain. Rob and I continued back up the river to the slip where Richard was waiting to retrieve the boat and get her back onto the stand as quickly as possible. This done we settled back into three days of contact with the public and with an estimated 30,000 people attending we were delighted with the outcome. We felt we had got off to a really good start.

Our next big planned event was entry in The Great River Race, a 22 mile dash from Richmond to Greenwich on the River Thames in London. This was due to take place the following Saturday and would be our boat's first real test. However, before I tell you about this I will take a few moments to explain the rationale behind the boat name.

Some weeks before the launch, when the boat was beginning to take shape and no longer looked like a pile of plywood, I thought it time to address the problem of a means of transporting the boat around the country. I mentioned the discussions I had with RM Trailers in a previous chapter but the name of the boat is inextricably linked with the acquisition of the trailer.

I am a member of the Worcester Business Breakfast Club and another regular member at that time was a chap called Trevor Lloyd-Adams, who managed Crowngate, the main shopping complex in Worcester city centre. I invited him for a cup of coffee and asked if he would be willing to pay for the trailer in return for the Crowngate logo on the boat. I had decided to 'sell off' spaces roughly 2 feet square for £2,000 in cash or kind. Trevor agreed and we then chatted about the wider project and boat name. He suggested, in order to try and raise awareness and more importantly ownership of our entry (on which basis most of our local support was likely to come), it would be appropriate to name her 'The Spirit of Worcester'. I thought this was an excellent suggestion but felt that with the Hospice involvement across the whole of South Worcestershire, it would be better to broaden the name to embrace the whole county. I ran this past Rob, who was happy with the idea but thought it would make it harder to raise support in his locality. As it happened very little was forthcoming from Cumbria in the end for various reasons, but in our experience it would have been extremely hard to have run a dual sponsorship campaign in two different locations some 200 miles apart. It is probably good advice to concentrate your efforts on one location and do that well. For our bid I had most of the contacts and fundraising expertise, and therefore most of this side of the project fell to me. In other circumstances, if I had a rowing partner I did not really know, I would probably enter into some kind of agreement where each party was responsible for an equal share of sponsorship acquisition. I am sure that some of the other teams handled things in this manner. Norman Butler, my good friend and fellow ocean rower, a guy who should be admired for his sheer guts and determination to continue against the odds, had real problems securing a committed partner and often it seemed there were plenty of people up for the idea but somewhat reticent when it came to putting money behind their enthusiasm. Norman had three different partners prior to the race and had to withdraw from the 2001 race due to resulting financial problems, but having had his race fees refunded by the Challenge Business he pressed on to complete a trans-Atlantic row from La Gomera under his own steam with the assistance of the ORS. He was going to go solo but managed to pick up a partner who was a reserve rower for one of the other CB race teams in Tenerife. Some 300 miles from his destination in Barbados his final partner had had enough and was taken off by a passing yacht leaving Norman to finish his crossing alone. I have become more and more convinced that it is this type of determination necessary to become an ocean rower whether or not you end up succeeding in your ultimate goal. Initially the big financial commitment can help sort out the men from the boys, but I really would advise anyone doing a row with one or more partners that you formally agree who is responsible for what from the start and stick to it as best you can.

Chapter Six

September 4th, 1999, was a significant day for the crew of the 'Spirit of Worcestershire'. Our brand new boat, built with our own fair hands, sat on the trailer behind Rob's car as we tentatively towed her down the M40 towards London, where we would participate in the Great River Race. The car and trailer were not that much shorter than an articulated lorry, so we proceeded with great care.

The Great River Race had been the next major goal following the launch and would be our first opportunity to test the boat's handling over a reasonable period of time. The fact that it was also a competition with many other competitors was an added bonus.

The Great River Race is a 22 mile bash down the River Thames from Richmond to Greenwich, held annually. Some 250 'traditional' rowing boats take part, from Cornish Gigs to Chinese Dragonboats, Shallops to Skiffs, Wherries to War Canoes, not to mention the occasional Atlantic Rowing Boat! There are various rules surrounding the race: no sliding seats, a cox and crewmember on each boat in addition to the rowers, of which there must be at least two; a flag must be flown and a number clearly displayed for boat recognition purposes.

The actual race was due to take place on the Sunday, but provision had been made for hardy souls to arrive the night before and camp in a field near the start, where a marquee had been set up and in which we would be both fed and entertained. The promise of a hearty breakfast before the start next morning was also something to look forward to.

Once we eventually arrived in London, found the river and what appeared to be the start, we looked around for assistance. Some kind of official or informed individual would have been helpful, but all we could find were portable toilets and the paraphernalia that alluded to some kind of event happening at some undisclosed time in the future or, God forbid, the past…….. no, the details we had been sent clearly stated that the race was on the following day! We decided to hang around for a while in case someone 'official' turned up but as the day wore on it was clear that the Great River Race 'officials' had joined the ranks of extinct species. Eventually we found a launch site, not really a slipway as such, but adequate to get the boat in the river. We rowed over to the opposite bank where we deduced a pontoon was available to moor the boat overnight, a fact confirmed by a local. The next job was to take the trailer to Greenwich, where the instructions told us a secure area had been designated for towing vehicles and trailers to be left, so boats could be retrieved at the finish of the race by the rowing teams. My son John and nephew David were acting as Cox and passenger and we left them with the tents to set up camp whilst Rob and I set off across the capital.

We found the secure area after some difficulty, compounded by having 25 feet of boat and trailer behind the car. Allegedly, the organisers had arranged for a mini bus at the allotted hour to transport us back to the campsite, or at least that's what it had said in the race blurb. The small crowd of fellow competitors gathering at the entrance was testimony to this fact, not to mention the confirmation we had sent to the organisers in advance of the event to say we would require this service. However, an impending sense of doom was beginning to settle upon us, particularly as the allotted hour passed by and no minibus appeared. Race HQ was not contactable for a reason I have now forgotten but eventually someone with a mobile phone and a little help from the security guard, managed to contact an organiser! It must have felt like the sense of excitement experienced at the discovery of the Coelacanth! An organiser yippee!

In fairness to the individual in question they did eventually arrange for taxis to transport us back to Richmond. What became of the mini bus no one will ever know. David and John had sorted the tents out and after a visit to the local we had some food from the bar-b-que, listened to the band for a while and then turned in to try and get some sleep before the next day's events.

After what transspired to be a poor night's sleep we had breakfast, an interesting fry up that would have sent a sports nutritionist into a flat spin, especially before a competitive event! By now, however, our experience was leading us to conclude that this race should not be taken too seriously. We packed up our gear, got a lift across the river and loaded up the boat. It was a beautiful day and we rowed across to the start for a pre-race inspection by the race judges. The scene was in complete contrast to the previous day, boats of all shapes and sizes everywhere, a start line, hundreds of people, rowers, boat and support crews, race officials (yes, even race officials!) and many spectators.

We had quite a long wait during which we registered, got our start time, race number (24) and even had a race official take a lively interest in our boat when he realised it was of the Atlantic breed. It transpired, though, that certain misdemeanours had occurred with an Atlantic boat entry in the past. Rumour has it that the boat in question, whilst starting the race with secured sliding seats experienced a failure of the lashings on route and the rowers suddenly found the seats moving! Unfortunately for those in question this contravention of the rules was spotted by race officials and led to some debacle, the outcome of which has been lost in the mists of time. I don't think it led to disqualification though.

Surprise! Surprise! The race judge wanted to view our boat and check the sliding seats! Fortunately Rob had made a very substantial construction that to the uninitiated looked like two piles of wood nailed together with normal sliding rowing seats perched on the top. These had been constructed over the normal seat rails and even the old boy checking them out seemed satisfied that only a torpedo was likely to move them.

There was one other Atlantic boat in the race, this with a bunch of young lads from a school on board. They set off before us and beat us, but I think this may have been because they were all rowing in shifts, rotating the crew and giving each other a regular rest. This is permitted within the rules. John and David hadn't come to row and a short spell on the oars half way down the course proved that this had been a wise decision! Anyway each of the 250 boats participating is given a handicap and the start is staggered, the theory being that if everybody rows at the same rates they should all finish together, thus making the final placing of each boat about right. Atlantic boats aren't really built for speed in this context so we were allocated a starting time very near the beginning of the start procedure. We headed off down river enjoying the spectacle and occasion. It was very hot and sunny which made the rowing more of an effort but made the race through the heart of London a very memorable affair. We did our best, enjoyed the feel of the boat under us and entered into the spirit of the race with plenty of amusing banter with fellow competitors as they passed us, or we passed them, on the way to the finish. Some of the boats were absolutely beautiful and a feast to the eye of anyone who appreciates the line of a well-built boat propelled at speed by a dedicated crew.

We pressed on past many London landmarks; the section past the House of Parliament, HMS Belfast and under Tower Bridge was particularly enjoyable. Tower Bridge marked the limit of the bridges and the river took on a much bigger feel as we made our way to Greenwich. We were also beginning to feel a bit tired, very hot and a mite sweaty by this point. We were glad to finally hear the finishing gun fire as we crossed the line and made our way to a pontoon, so that we could disembark,

Rob & the author approaching Tower Bridge on the race's last leg.

get the car and trailer and make our way home. Unfortunately over 50 other boats of various shapes and sizes were all trying to do the same thing, which was fair enough as we all had homes to go to! But the prize idiot in his Plastic Gin Palace was something I had not bargained for. Rob and the boys had gone to collect the car and our race certificates, leaving me to tend the boat. As you will appreciate she had only been launched a week ago and the potential for fairly significant damage at this point was considerable. The boats surrounding me had fenders but there was a lot of movement from the river and it was as much as I could do to keep them away from impending disaster. I don't know what else the organisers could do but a serious look at the finish and getting people off the water in an orderly way without boat damage would not go amiss. The situation was just about bearable until 'the idiot' arrived. From whence he came I do not know, unless he was ferrying people from the old sailing ship marking the finish line. He was 'in charge' of a large motor cruiser which was trying to get alongside the pontoon to drop people off. Large heavy cruiser and pontoon with small wooden rowing boats in between is not a good mix at the best of times, but did this bother Hooray Henry? Not on your life. This prize idiot kept coming despite our objections and eventually forced his way in, rowing boats, including ours, being hurriedly moved to either side, an almost impossible feat given the congestion. It nearly caused major damage to our brand new boat and in the end, despite being a mild mannered sort of guy, my apprehension boiled over and I gave him a mouthful! The fact that he had been allowed anywhere near the pontoon at that time was grossly unfair on the rowers and should have been dealt with by the organisers. If the boat had been ferrying people to and from the finish ship and was part of the organisation of the race then shame on you, you deserve the black spot! As for Hooray Henry himself, I suggest next time he is out for a jolly, he might like to park his palace by a quay at a car ferry port and when the ferry comes in see how he feels as it is crushed to pieces against the harbour wall! On second thoughts such a scenario might do us all a favour!

Anyway, enough of my moaning, apart from the problems at the start and finish, on the whole the Great River Race was a positive and enjoyable experience and gave us the opportunity to test the boat for the first time. She performed well and we were impressed with the result of our handiwork. We were placed 148th in the fleet of 233 entries and completed the 22 mile course in four hours 13 minutes and 22 seconds. Considering this was our first run in the 'Spirit' we were pleased with this result.

During the next seven weeks between the Great River Race and the next significant event in the journey towards our trans Atlantic adventure, several events took place which seem to become almost mundane as the days rolled into weeks, the weeks into months and on into years. On Sunday, September 19th, I went to a posh school in Malvern to speak at a regular Sunday Forum meeting to tell them about the race. My address was greeted with polite interest! The following Sunday was marked by a trip to Chester for a training update and assessment, the usual VO2 max agony and all that. The next day I attended a Hospice fund raiser at the Guildhall in Worcester, and on Sunday, October 3rd, I took the boat to feature outside Cannons Health Club for their open day. This event is designed to attract new members, and my involvement was part of my side of the deal we had struck, which entitled me to free membership, so that I could use their facilities to train, in exchange for all the PR stuff I could achieve for the Club. In my diary for the next weekend I have an entry saying 'Kent furniture'. My parents live in Kent and we must have been shifting some furniture to or from their house….who knows? But as it isn't central to the story, I will move swiftly on!

A guy called Will Mason had contacted me who was thinking of entering the race and wanted to come to look at our boat and chat about the race and our experience so far. He duly arrived the following weekend and spent some time chatting about the challenge. Rob and I had planned a training run the next weekend on Ullswater, in the Lake District, and invited Will to come up and join us. Unfortunately he couldn't, but said his Dad would like to come and meet us and see the boat so we arranged for him to make contact at our proposed launch site the following Saturday. Little did we then know what was in store for us!

I left for the Lakes early on the Saturday morning and covered the 200 miles to our rendezvous at Glenridding on the banks of Ullswater with ease. The nine mile long lake is second only to Windermere in size, but its long, twisting outline provides a variety of scenery unsurpassed by any other lake in this beautiful part of England. Glenridding lies at the southern end of the lake, which is surrounded by high crags; some days the water can be smooth as glass but on wild days, when summer's balmy embrace is but a memory, the crags act as a funnel, accelerating the wind to an angry winter blast. Unfortunately for us it was on such a day that we arrived on Ullswater's tempestuous shore. We prepared the boat for launching and Will's Dad turned up. He seemed a really nice bloke and we chatted as he helped us prepare. I think his errand was to suss out what this race was all about, gauge whether or not we were sane, have a look at the boat and build some kind of confidence so he could return to Will's Mum and re assure her that if Will did undertake a race entry there was a vague possibility that her little boy might return from the briny deep rather than ending up at the bottom of the Abyssal Plain! I think he went away feeling he had achieved some success, but I am pretty certain he was unconvinced with regard to our sanity, or the lack of it. As Rob and I pulled out into a howling wind and generally very unpleasant conditions perhaps the feeling was somewhat mutual!

The icy northerly wind was blowing straight up the lake. Just below Glenridding lies a small island; the water to the left of this looked quite shallow but once we had left the lee of the land at the top of the lake there was nothing to stop it affecting our progress. We suddenly found ourselves at the mercy of its awesome power and shot off as it pushed us from behind. Then it caught us on the quarter and swung us beam on to the wind. No matter how hard we tried we could not bring her back on course, so found ourselves being blown down the lake sideways towards the island. We were able to set the boat up to pass the island to starboard. If we had tried leaving it to port, we would have foundered as the wind would have pushed us onto the shore faster than we could have cleared it. The left hand passage looked very shallow and I hoped there was sufficient depth to take our minimal draft. Thankfully we passed safely and once this was accomplished without going aground we rowed like mad to the right hand side of the lake to find some shelter from the wind. We were relieved to come under the lee of the hills on this side of the lake, which enabled us to regain control of the boat and proceed with the wind astern that greatly helped, rather than hindered our progress. If you look at a map of Ullswater you will see that the first two miles lie almost exactly on a north south axis, which could be described as the 'axis of evil' if the wind is blowing hard from the south as was the case with us. Heading north you reach Silver Point where the lake turns to the NE, once past the Point the hills afford some protection from a wild southerly as you leave the acceleration zone behind you. The plan had been to try a two-hour on two-hour off shift system, which we understood to be the preferred choice of successful teams in the last race. I had been looking forward to a starry, moonlit night, with glassy black water and the kind of silence only isolation can bring. We intended to row back and forth up and down the lake for a 24 hour period and go home in the satisfied knowledge that we had achieved our goal. As the first sheets of rain hard driven by the relentless wind chased us up the lake any illusion of this tranquil imagery was shattered. We decided that our plan would be impossible to follow and so pulled into Howtown, moored to a private jetty, took out our Seacook gimballed stove for a brew and made a decision as to what to do next.

Howtown lies about half way down Ullswater, but the problem with Howtown is its location. Situated in a large bay, the axis once again runs North to South, with Fusedale and Howe Grain running up from the shore and providing two more gaps between the hills and the inevitable acceleration zone for the wind (acceleration zones are found all over the world, the Canary Islands are renowned for this phenomenon where the wind is squeezed between two major objects, like mountains or Islands and thus accelerates to a far greater speed than the normal average creating severe local weather conditions).

Rob usually took charge of the cooking, something that had always been the case on our various expeditions in the past, it was just one of those many unspoken understandings that developed over many years of friendship. As the water was set to boil, the next squall descended upon us. We could see it coming down the valley driven hard by the gale force wind. It was made even more spectacular by the sleet now mixed into the rain, which came in huge sheets silhouetted against the dramatic background of green and brown mountainsides. The angry grey scudding clouds released their torment upon us as if to say any mere human with an ounce of self respect would be sat in front of a warm log fire behind closed doors as the elements lashed the window panes taunting those within. I repaired to the bow storage space, just big enough to get inside, and watched Rob getting wetter and wetter as he tended the stove. We had a wonderfully comforting hot drink that washed down some inadequate snack bars. We then made the decision to row back up to Glenridding before dark and moor up to the jetty for the night. We decided not to head to Pooley Bridge at the North end of the lake because we would never have been able to get the boat back up the lake in these conditions and were not at all sure that there was a suitable place to retrieve the boat onto the trailer.

We cast off and began what was to become one of the hardest challenges had ever faced in all the mad exploits we had done together over the years. As we rowed back down the lake we realised just how fast we had been going with the assistance of the wind on our way up. The opposite was now true and every stroke only seemed to propel the boat about half a length. It was hard work, but had the benefit of warming our tired and aching bodies. The sleet was relentless, as was the wind, and we could not afford to stop for a moment as we would have lost the hard won ground already covered. Slowly but surely we made our way towards Silver Point, but I remained anxious about the couple of miles beyond this landmark. Not only would this be the hardest row of the day but also, as we were already tired and cold, there would be no room for error or any opportunity to stop and rest. The rocky shore was not an option as the short steep waves and sharp rocks would have made short work of our 9 mm plywood hull. I have often said that at least in the open ocean there is little to bump into apart from passing ships, the odd submerged container that has fallen from some distant hull and the occasional tree trunk or the like, but here everything offered only a short distance from disaster, and it was so cold!

Eventually Silver Point loomed large on our port bow. We rounded it as close as possible and bang, the wind hit us again. I had hoped it might ease with the onset of night, but no such luck. To begin with we seemed to be standing still and the only course of action was to pull even harder, a choice we just didn't want to entertain. Unfortunately we had no option but to up the effort. I don't know how we did it, considering we were dehydrated, cold, tired and hungry, but it is these personal acts of heroism in fairly desperate circumstances that, if you survive, form the basis for real bonds of lasting friendship and, to be honest, make life worth living in our cotton wool society that lacks adventure, challenge and a certain element of risk. I use the word 'heroic' reservedly; you may consider the whole enterprise somewhat foolhardy and if so perhaps you have never pushed yourself to the limit, I'm not saying that you should but when you do, I think it takes you to a new level of understanding and experience, which may be what this whole thing is all about.

I distinctly remember golden leaves floating motionless on the surface of the lake, here we were pulling for all we were worth, every stroke representing a huge effort and those blasted leaves were hardly moving, clearly demonstrating that we were doing little more than standing still as the wind laughed in our faces. More power, more energy, neither Rob nor I said anything but instinctively knew what we had to do. Gradually, with the light fading, we worked even harder and began to make more progress. The worst thing to do at this stage, however, was to look over your shoulder to see how much nearer the Glenridding jetty was; it never seemed to get any closer. This was now as much a mental battle as a physical one as the cold and the wet searched out every nook and cranny of our being. We did make the jetty in the end after over an hour's painful rowing to cover the last mile. It was dark and cold, the sleet continued to lash down and, if anything, the wind had strengthened. Even mooring the boat was a challenge; this was my job as Rob's usual attempts at knots and the like more often than not ended up with the object being tied disappearing in the direction of the current! I was so cold, but realised that a really good job was necessary as the boat was broadside on to the wind that whipped under the jetty and tried to push us back the way we had come.

Once the boat was safe it was time to find some dry clothes and try to get warm. By this time I was shivering uncontrollably and knew that if I didn't do something fairly radical soon, hypothermia would set in and I'd be in real trouble. My dry clothes were in the car about five minutes walk away, I made it and stripped off which didn't seem to make a lot of difference to how I felt, if anything it felt warmer with the weather on my skin. I towelled down and put on the dry stuff but still didn't really feel any warmer. We repaired to the pub and ordered a hot meal and a couple of pints. Just to underline our state, we finished neither which is totally unprecedented on our normal expeditions. We were starting to feel a little warmer but when we left the pub for the boat the severe shivering started again. I hated it. Finally I was able to creep into my down sleeping bag inside the little cabin on the boat. We battened down the hatches and for the first time I began to feel real warmth again. I began to enjoy hearing the wind howling outside and the sleet hammering on the cabin roof. In this state of relaxed bliss I pondered the day's events, and, now it was all over, began to appreciate what we had achieved. It had been a real test for the boat and our own resolve, surely an episode that would stand us in good stead for what lay ahead.

Chapter Seven

I was filled with a sense of anticipation as I made my way through the mayhem of Heathrow traffic to the short stay car park. For quite some time I had been looking forward to the arrival of a certain Alby McCracken from Australia. I had never actually met him before, our previous contact having been via the Internet and telephone.

I can't really remember how I originally found out about the item of equipment of which Alby is probably the world expert, an item that I would not go to sea without and would suggest that any ocean rower should get hold of for their 'must have' equipment list.

My son John had designed a sign for me to hold at arrivals with a picture of Australia and the Australian flag accompanying Alby's name. I didn't really know what to expect but I thought the sign would enable us to make contact. It's a funny business as weary passengers flood out of arrivals and you stand there looking for someone you think might fit the mental picture you have built of the person you are about to meet. I didn't expect him to be wearing a bush hat with corks hanging from it but that might have aided the process! Eventually Alby appeared, a thick set, stocky guy, somewhat more advanced in years than me, whose complexion looked like it was used to the outdoor life. It was the first time Alby had been to Europe. He was on his way to the Amsterdam Boat Show, sponsored by the Victorian Government. He had offered to make a detour to the UK to give us one of his products and demonstrate how to use it. In return I had offered to pick him up and take him up to the Lake District to meet Rob, experience a good pub meal, some nice warm beer, have a trip in the boat and see a bit of this beautiful part of the country before returning to Heathrow and his onward flight to the Netherlands.

We immediately hit it off as we loaded his gear into the boot of my car and started the long journey North. We talked about all sorts of things as the miles passed by, not least Alby's business, Paraanchors Australia. For many years Alby had been designing and making Parachute Anchors for all sorts of applications from leisure craft to the fishing industry. The chutes range in size from a few feet in diameter to huge 100 foot monsters. Alby recounted with some amusement a testing session at the local airfield: having secured the 100 foot chute to a 4 x 4 vehicle, they had inflated it but the power of the chute was so great that it proceeded to drag the vehicle down the tarmac even though all the brakes were on!

Parachute anchors are far more superior to a drogue and Alby has covered all the essential information about the product on his website (www.paraanchors.com.au) From my experience of using the one he supplied, and the information he gave me before leaving for the race, I would suggest the following for any would be user in a boat of about seven metres in length and roughly a tonne when fully laden. A seven foot parachute would be adequate but Alby recommended nine foot, which is what we took. Rumour has it that the Kiwi team did extensive tests and took a 12 foot chute but you would have to ask them if this is correct. I personally think that is overkill, but each to their own! The chute is attached to a 120 metre length of three strand nylon line with a stretching capacity of 50% when fully loaded. This takes out any snatching and makes for a far more comfortable ride in heavy weather. In Rob Hamil's book he cut this length to 70 metres, but Alby reckoned that this was far too short and would set up uncomfortable snatching which could present problems with wavelengths. The line need only be 8 mm; I took 12 mm which was really unnecessary and added to the weight. 10 mm is quite sufficient for a belt and braces job but it does need to have the stretch. In the light of experience the length could be cut to 100 metres but I would argue no less. On the other side of the chute a weight is attached, I used a heavy stainless steel bow shackle; for larger boats Alby recommends a short length of anchor chain. A 15 metre length of water ski line is attached to the weight and at the other end of the line a small buoy which floats on the surface. This arrangement keeps the chute between 10-15 metres below the surface, which is about right for the thing to work efficiently. Alby then suggests that a 20 metre ski line be attached to the buoy and then on to a second similar buoy at the other end. Once the heavy weather is passed the idea is to take your boat to the second buoy and pick it up, pull up the line and surface buoy which deflates the chute and makes it easy to retrieve. However, this doesn't really work for the ocean rower as you have to row up to the buoy, into the weather. I spoke to Alby after I returned and would now recommend a larger buoy be used at the end of the first line from the chute and a second length of ski line tied to the buoy and run right back to the boat to act as a tripping line. When you want to retrieve the chute all you have to do is pull in this line and the chute will collapse and be pulled in with ease. By now you may be very confused, so I suggest you look at the Para Anchors website where the above arrangements are illustrated. My apologies for swaying between imperial and metric measurements I guess it's just my age!

There are two major advantages of a parachute anchor. First of all when deployed it will more or less hold you on station, unlike a drogue which will keep your head to wind but you lose ground as the weather sweeps by. Secondly, if the weather is going in the opposite direction to the one in which you wish to go, but there is a current under the surface, a parachute anchor is powerful enough to pull you in your chosen direction or at least counteract the effect of wind. Anyway, the best thing to do is get one and try it, you won't be disappointed if you have set it up correctly and it may just save your life!

Alby and I eventually arrived at Rob's place in Appleby. It had been a long day and we were both glad to have reached our destination. Alby was in remarkable form considering that he had been travelling constantly since leaving Oz a lifetime ago. After a brief interlude to wash and change, Alby produced the parachute he had made for us: it was a work of art. As this stranger from the other side of the world told us about the chute, its construction and use, it seemed as though we had known him for years. Time and again on the long road of preparation for this great adventure we would meet many more 'Albys', people who shared our enthusiasm and sense of purpose, people who were prepared to get their hands dirty and muck in, share encouragement and friendship. I reckon there lies the paradox of ocean rowing: the execution of the row is a fairly individual affair, especially if you take on a solo

The author's good friend, Alby McCracken, just before going out on Ullswater.

challenge, but in order to get to sea in the first place it takes a small army of supporters. You really do meet an awful lot of really good people like Alby.

After a while we repaired to a local hostelry and ate and drank the evening away. The next morning we took the boat to Ullswater and launched her in much more favourable conditions than our last encounter with this great old lake! We took Alby out with us, so he could experience the boat first hand, which he seemed to enjoy. Rob then took the boat back to Appleby while Alby and I set off for Worcester, taking us through the heart of the Lakes in all its magnificence. Once outside the Lake District it was back on the M6 and a stark contrast to what went before. It was getting dark and the only other vaguely amusing part of the rest of the journey was when Alby decided to give his wife a call on the mobile. He rang and she answered the phone, "Hi Cracken!" he said. I'm not entirely sure what followed but without much more conversation Alby was apologising profusely due to the fact it was about 3 a.m. in Sale; the rest of the call was fairly short!

Alby stayed the night with us in Worcester and next morning announced that he didn't want to overdo our hospitality and insisted he got the train down to London and on to Heathrow for his flight to Holland. He said he wanted to experience a trip on the railway, perhaps he felt it was safer than my driving!

One of many WM Rowing Challenge events, this one with young people at Cannons in Worcester.

The end of the year was fast coming into view, but before 1999 ebbed away there was the small matter of the West Midlands Rowing Challenge. I previously alluded to this in an earlier chapter. Richard Lovell had worked very hard to set it all up and a number of groups in the region had registered. The idea was for teams of 24 to do a sponsored row in shifts using Concept 2 rowing machines. Richard had to go over to Nottingham on several weekends to pick up extra Concept 2 rowers for the purpose and a wide variety of teams had registered representing groups from schools, fitness clubs and local authorities. These teams took on the challenge throughout the month and I attended several of their events. We had offered a Concept 2 rowing machine as a prize, which was ultimately won by fitness club teams from Kidderminster. Everyone put a great deal of effort into the challenge, which gained a great deal of publicity. Unfortunately the overall fund raising total was somewhat disappointing, especially for Richard since he had done most of the work to organise the event.

Getting the money together for a row is probably one of the most painful things a would-be rower must endure. I say 'endure' because I found it a constant concern that pervaded everything. I didn't have any problem with doing my utmost to give sponsors and donors as much value for money as possible once they had given their support, but getting there was a big uphill struggle. Having talked at some length to other teams, this is not an unusual experience. Whilst there is always plenty of advice it is generally pretty unhelpful, though well meaning. If the question begins 'Have you tried?', you can generally bet that you have and that the response is predictable. Here are a few standard responses to requests for support, I'll leave you to think up your own interpretations: -

- "We have allocated all our sponsorship and charitable funding from this year's budget."
- "We judge all requests against strict criteria and we are afraid your request does not meet them."
- "We wish you well in your challenge."
- "We only support local organisations."
- "We cannot help financially but if you would like to contact .... we would be glad to donate some of our products" (OK as long as they aren't a sofa manufacturer! Having said that your request may be a little naïve as the link between sofas and ocean rowing is a little tenuous!).

The real problem with all of the above is the boring predictability of such responses and their frequency. You will have to write hundreds of letters, make countless phone calls and probably attend several fruitless meetings. These are the worst of the lot because if you get to the point of a face-to-face encounter your spirits rise and you feel that at last someone is listening and interested. It is very much more likely that if you do get this far you will achieve a result, but if you don't the financial clouds that gather over your project seem blacker than ever. I remember one occasion with a company in Worcester: they contacted me after seeing a press article and expressed interested in supporting the project, requesting further information. I spent a considerable amount of time and resources to put together a bespoke package with a view to a meeting. I delivered it personally but then heard nothing more. I made phone calls and wrote follow up letters. Eventually I had a letter that read as though I had made the initial contact and they weren't interested. This sort of thing makes the whole process even more frustrating, especially when you have been contacted and your hopes raised by someone who ultimately doesn't even have the courtesy to respond positively to a request they made in the first place!

I would argue it is unusual to get a main sponsor who will fund the whole project. It is not impossible, though, as a few have achieved this in the past. You may get a boat title holder, and it would appear the going rate for this is around £10,000, but that does present you with a bit of a problem as a budget row will probably cost you at least four times that; if you are offering boat branding which you have already 'sold' to your title holder you may find the next £30,000 a bit difficult if your branding space has been used up. Gifts in kind are a great way of lowering the need for cash and you should also try for a trade account with chandlers etc that can save you up to 60% on your bills. We set up a company with the Hospice that meant VAT (Value Added Tax @17.5% in the UK) could be re claimed. The only word of caution on that is the fact that you have to add it on when you come to sell your boat afterwards, which may make it less competitive if there are several other teams trying to sell their craft at the same time.

In the end a regional campaign probably works the best. You will need plenty of time. Make a list of all potential contacts, your employer, their clients and partners organisations and clubs you relate to, family, friends and relations, you will be surprised by how many people you know who might help. Organise lots of fund raising events but don't over estimate what they may yield. If you expect the worst you may be pleasantly surprised. Always be up front about what you are doing with the money you raise, especially if you have linked up with a charitable cause. Is it for the project costs or the work of the charity, what percentage goes to what? People are happy to give if they are clear about the aims; the last thing you want is some media scandal about misappropriated funds. It is good to put together a written agreement at the start to avoid confusion if a problem arises.

Suffice to say funding is a long journey and probably the most difficult of all the aspects of an ocean row. One day the sport will be properly recognised and major sponsorship could follow, but the down side of this could be to narrow the hugely diverse nature of those who go down to the sea to row.

Ultimately you will need to engage in local fund raising events, which can be very enjoyable, and you will also overcome the knock backs from letters refusing your requests as your sponsorship targets begin to be achieved. However when a guy comes all the way from the other side of the world, takes the time to meet a couple of strangers in a foreign land and give them some of the fruit of his labour, which could ultimately save their lives, you begin to understand that there is more to 'sponsorship' than first meets the eye. Strangers become friends, and sponsorship becomes an indication of a belief that the individual or organisation concerned will achieve the required goal, then the whole thing enters a new phase. I guess it was people like Alby McCracken, from Sale, Victoria, Australia, who made the whole thing worthwhile.

Chapter Eight

T he new Millennium dawned amidst spectacular celebrations around the world. Once again Australia seemed to be ahead of the game but our little effort in Worcester hit the spot so far as we were concerned. Looking at that year's diary, the majority of recorded activity seems to have been an endless cycle of training interspersed with the occasional visit to a boat show, with an organised Challenge Business event to address some aspect of the race. The first of these was on Friday, January 14th, at the London Boat Show. I can't remember the exact subject of the day but they were always reasonably well attended, including competitors from overseas, and addressed issues that were of some help to the general organisation of each team.

Because there had been so much activity to build and finish the boat (to a basic specification), keep the finance flowing and achieve the initial goals set for this early part of the project, the itinerary for the year 2000 looked a little barren at first glance. We could have been forgiven for being lulled into a false sense of security but the count down to the start kept ticking relentlessly on, as someone once said, 'time and tide wait for no man'.

If I were to split the 3.5 years of preparation into chunks it would look something like this: -

1998: Speculation and registration followed by a flurry of activity to meet the initial financial deadlines and make general preparations for building the boat.

1999: Build and launch the boat, then fit her out to a standard that would enable us to start training in sheltered waters against a background of sponsorship, fundraising, publicity and promotion.

2000: Continued the process of fundraising, promotion and training.

It is the latter upon which I intend to focus in this chapter.

I must warn you at this point that some of this will get a bit technical for those of you who have never tackled such a specific programme in a gym, but I will try and give a bit of explanation as I go along, trying not to be too patronising, nerdy or boring! A point to remember is that prior to the challenge I had never frequented a gym or embarked on a formal training programme with professional support. Whilst I was in reasonable shape all my previous experience had been as a result of practical involvement in the sports that maintained my interest on an occasional basis, namely walking (back packs, waterproofs and tents, not just down to the chip shop!), cycling and kayaking.

Earlier in the text I recounted the story of the pile of sand in Rob's garden that ultimately led to our association with University College Chester offering help, support and training programmes in return for us becoming research guinea pigs and the subject of a PhD. The relationship worked well and we built a good rapport with the various members of the Sports Science Team, as the weeks grew into months and the months became years. By the end of it we were very fit and strong so I guess it must have worked. In hindsight we should have paid far more attention to the mental side of our preparation, and the outcome of our nutritional programme, in the form of the food we took on the boat, was very poor. Both of these areas I will tackle later on but I would counsel any would be ocean rower to seek advice and really thoroughly prepare ALL three major areas.

Training doesn't stop there either. There is navigation, general seamanship, the weather, tides, winds and currents, communications, sea survival, emergency procedures, first aid and other matters medical, not to mention developing an intimate knowledge of your gear and equipment (including what to do if it gives up on you). However, it's the physical stuff I will embark upon describing now.

I guess the two areas a physiological training programme tries to address are strength and endurance. An athlete can be highly trained to walk or run long distances competitively; he or she may be very lean, nimble and fast, but given a weight to carry as well things may be very different. Ranulph Fiennes reports that two of his expeditions failed because of this; members were very fit aerobically, but lacked the necessary strength for the challenge. This is where specific training for the particular event you intend to undertake is essential, and may make the difference between success and failure. In our case the team wanted to sort out our aerobic fitness before concentrating on the strength aspects of the programme. So in the beginning there was aerobics!

Aerobic exercise develops heart and lung capacity, I think it goes something like this: if you aren't fit your lungs absorb much smaller amounts of oxygen than does a fit person. Once this oxygen is absorbed into the blood it needs to be transported to your muscles where it is used to power your activity. In an unfit person the heart may pump at say 100 beats per minute but pretty inefficiently, in other words, small amounts of absorbed oxygen are transported in the blood to weak muscles, which in turn don't convert this vital fuel very well. If you suddenly want to work hard the body is ill prepared and the heart has to work harder and harder for far less benefit than in someone who has trained their body to work better through correct diet and exercise. If you neglect yourself as so often is the case in our present day society all sorts of nasty things happen inside through lack of use and the wrong fuel, which eventually leads to your 'engine', conking out! As you do more exercise and use your 'internal engine', more oxygen is absorbed into your blood and your heart is able to pump greater volumes around the body even if the heart rate remains the same, in other words you become more efficient. What often happens is that the heart rate decreases but its activity is far more effective hence it works less hard for greater effect. This is what training and good health is all about. In fact efficiency is the key to good training and in the case of the ocean rower good preparation, efficiency and a large dollop of good fortune in all aspects of a row is the key to success.

Aerobic exercise develops heart and lung capacity, anaerobic exercise is something else! In fact the dictionary defines it as 'capable of existing in the absence of air and oxygen'. This happens when you do short sharp workouts with weights, fast sprints or on the rowing machine. If you have ever tried doing a 2,000 metre row on a Concept 2 machine as fast as you can, you will understand what it feels like, I would imagine death is a more pleasant experience! Basically anaerobic exercise kicks in when you have used up the absorbed oxygen supply in your blood and you keep going for a short period until you can't go on any longer. It's when your body screams with pain and exhaustion and your muscles fill up with Lactic Acid, which causes the pain and the general stiffness the next day! Another benefit of training is to limit the time it takes your body to recover after hard physical exercise. Ocean Rowing is largely a low intensity sport, unless you are in danger or an emergency situation when you have to give everything to survive, but because it depends on the rower doing constant work over very long periods of time, the ability to maximise recovery in the short rest periods between rowing shifts is essential. Handling a boat in one of the most extreme and hostile environments in the world, which can weigh anything up to a tonne fully laden, needs strength and endurance. Another interesting thing about Ocean Rowing is that you are probably best aiming to reach peak fitness during the row rather than at the start, something that can be attained because of the nature and length of the activity. I am no expert in this field and can only go by my own experience of working with the sports scientists over a couple of years, with very specific training programmes, so if you disagree with some of this I don't mind as healthy debate can only be good for the sport overall. We also did a lot of work on nutrition, namely whether a high carbohydrate or fat diet would best suit the nature of the challenge. I'll come back to this later.

So what did the specific nature of our training programmes entail? We started a disciplined regime at the beginning of 1999, with each week being split into four sessions with three rest days breaking things up. So Week One started on March 8th, and looked like this: -

Note: spm = strokes per minute on a Concept 2 rowing machine or 'ergo' as it is also known (on an ocean row you probably do about 18–24spm on average in reasonable conditions).

bpm = heart beats per minute, which is measured by wearing a heart rate monitor and helps to regulate the effort you are putting into your exercise.

Each session started with a general warm up and stretch for about five minutes and similar warm down at the end.

Monday: 1000m warm up @22spm > 2000m@36spm > 2000m@22spm > a 20 minute cycle.

Tuesday: Rest

Wednesday: 2000m warm up @22spm > 20 minute cycle > Weights session 1 (I'll explain in a minute).

Thursday: Rest

Friday: 1000m warm up @22spm > 20 minute run @ 133 bpm > Body weight circuit.

Saturday: 1000m warm up @22spm > 5000m @32spm > weights session 2

Sunday: Rest

With each programme lasting eight weeks we were given a weights programme. Session One above went like this: -

All 3x15 repetitions: -

1. Lateral Pull down
2. Seated Row
3. Leg extensions
4. Half squats
5. Crunches

We only had two combinations at the beginning, and Session 2 looked like this: -

1. Pec Fly
2. Chest Press
3. Shoulder Press
4. Leg Curls
5. Lunges

The body weight circuit above, something I didn't exactly look forward to, went like this: -

3 circuits of 30 seconds flat out on each exercise followed by 30 seconds rest: -

1. Press ups
2. Crunches
3. Lunges (left leg)
4. Underhand chin ups
5. Dorsal raises
6. Lunges (right leg)

I won't attempt to explain how you do all the above, if you are really into exercise you will already know, if you're not you probably won't want to, and if you are thinking about it you will know where to find out. Suffice to say, if you are about to embark on an ocean rowing project, see if you can persuade you local gym to support you with free membership in exchange for any PR benefits you can give. They will be able to instruct you on any exercises you are not sure of, or give you a programme if you haven't got the sort of support we had. I would also say it is worth contacting a university with a sports science department who may be able to help you like Chester did us. A local gym will give you a general fitness programme but you will probably need more specific 'professional' advice for a rowing project. If you have a local rowing club they may also be able to help and even support you in your quest but don't expect too much as they are going to be into rowing pencil shaped boats down rivers or other flat water, and may, therefore, find the concept of an ocean row in a one tonne boat over several thousand miles as alien as show jumping! My advice would be to pick and mix until you find the right combination. On the other hand you could just relax, take it easy and do like Jim Shekta says he did, when entering the 1997 Atlantic Rowing Race, and row a small pleasure boat around a lake in Europe for three months before leaving for the start!

By week 50, (April 24th) the sessions looked like this: -

Monday:	Rowing session 5
Tuesday:	Rowing session 6
Wednesday:	Rest
Thursday:	Rowing session 5
Friday:	Rowing session 6
Saturday:	Rest
Sunday:	Rowing session 5

Rowing session 5 by this time looked like this: -

- 10 minutes @ 20spm
- 5 minutes @ 22spm
- 5 minutes @ 24spm
- 5 minutes @ 20spm
- 5 minutes @ 24spm
- 5 minutes @ 22spm
- 10 minutes @ 20spm

Rowing session 6 looked like this: -

- 5 minutes @ 20spm
- 10 minutes @ 22spm
- 15 minutes @ 24spm
- 10 minutes @ 22spm
- 5 minutes @ 20 spm

All the above were done to cover as many metres as possible by the end of each segment. I would record the distance covered and try to exceed the previous work out by competing against myself, to make the whole thing a bit more interesting. Having said that I don't have a problem with spending long periods on an ergo like some people do. The week I have just outlined above was all rowing, but that two month programme also continued the weights sessions and a number of 'own choice' days with a body weight circuit and aerobic sessions from 30 minutes to an hour.

By the time the training programme was drawing to a close in September 2001, we were regularly doing 90 minute rows on the ergo and two hours on, two hours off, two hours on rows, alongside the aerobic and weight training sessions. I have a 37-hour contract at work, although I always seem to do more, but I negotiated a reduction to 30 hours in the final year to give more time for the training and preparations that were taking more and more time as the day of departure neared. Ocean rowing is not something you can engage in as a minor hobby, you need time and lots of it! Unless of course you do a double handed row and leave all the preparation to your partner but this is a recipe for potential conflict at a later date, which is why it is important to try and reach an agreement as to who is going to do what before you really get going in earnest. In our case we both followed the same training programme which developed a fellowship of suffering, so Rob and I were pretty clear about who was doing what.

Every two months the training programme was punctuated by a trip to Chester for assessment. We would go up for the day and do VO2 max tests and have all sorts of measurements taken to inform the research and see how we were progressing.

During the last year we did a few prolonged exercises. These included two 24 hour rows and a 48 hour session in the lab. We had to do these because the former was required to assess the effects of different diets and the latter to inform the research. Apparently only data from the controlled environment of the lab would be acceptable for research purposes. We also did an extended 24 hour row in the boat on Windemere, which was only partially successful on account of the fact that our radio communications didn't co-operate, and nor did our mobile phones!

I think the worst of these extended sessions was the 48 hour row. We had the ergo at one end of the lab with a TV to try and make it a little less boring although I must say some of the programmes would have been better ignored. I found the Welsh language output particularly hard to comprehend but to be honest once into the second 24 hour period the programmes could have been in any language! We did 2 hour on, two hour off sessions and kept the machine going all the time. After each session we had tests done on spit and urine, amongst other things, and were asked to eat specific quantities of food. At about 0300 hours on the Sunday morning I felt terrible and began throwing up as I tried to complete my shift, I wasn't going to give up but only completed a pathetic 6,000 metres in the second one hour period. By the last session I was back on form and did well in excess of 12,000. In total we managed over 480,000 metres over the two days which worked out as the equivalent of having rowed well into the North of Scotland; it felt like it too! By the time we got to Tenerife we were feeling ready for anything!

However, I did say I would address the whole psychological training we underwent. Well in short we didn't. We had a session with a sports psychologist at Chester but nothing really came of this and I can't say it really helped our preparations at all. In comparison with my friend Norman Butler, who rowed the course against the odds having withdrawn from the race and lost three rowing partners during his preparations, this area was very ill prepared. As far as I know, Norman had extensive psychological training and to great effect if the final result was anything to go by. The physical training did help psychologically, as it made you feel you were ready for what lay ahead and could achieve the challenge from a physical point of view, but ultimately I would argue that a high percentage of achieving success outside of all the setbacks you can experience in the form of the weather, injury and the physical environment, is down to what is in your head and your heart. If you are not prepared mentally for the enormity of the task, success may remain only a dream. One aspect of mental preparation I would highly recommend is trying to make time to get out in the boat on the sea in different situations, including overnight, and see how you get on. Do be careful, however, because the most hazardous part of any ocean row is generally accepted to be the first and last 100 miles, particularly when you get close to land. If you suddenly find the wind gets up and you are on a lee shore that could be the end of not only your training session but also your whole project, in a worst-case scenario that could include you. So for coastal or inshore training it is a good idea to arrange a support crew with a boat that can give you a tow if necessary and always check the weather forecast and local conditions. You might consider informing the coast guard of your prospective route, time of departure and ETA, and I would recommend that sea trials are only undertaken once your boat is fully equipped for sea, just in case you run into difficulties. If you are unprepared or take things on with a cavalier attitude you will probably get away with it, but you may contribute to bringing the sport into disrepute, quickly destroying the work that has gone on for many years to raise standards and take a more 'professional' approach. To underline this I would like to draw the attention of would be rowers to the fact that many countries now require strict standards to be met before granting permission for departure from their territorial waters. This is because they don't want to end up with rescue bills of tens of thousands of pounds, not to mention the unnecessary risks to their own emergency service personnel. The Ocean Rowing Society is working hard to keep the departure ports open to everyone who wishes to undertake an ocean rowing challenge. By advising on minimum standards gained through interaction with rowers and the relevant national authorities there is really no excuse these days to fail in this area. If a potential row ends at the point of departure it is probably because the rower(s) have not taken advantage of this wealth of experience or are unaware it exists. Of course it could be because the authorities don't think the project is adequately prepared. Whatever the reason, it will only take one bright spark (no reference to the boat of that name here guys!) to close the coasts for future and more responsible adventurers.

Finally, nutrition. We had quite a lot of attention paid to this area of our preparation. I said earlier that we undertook a comparative assessment of the dietary options for the row. This entailed a two week period on a high fat diet followed by a 24 hour row, then a week on a 'normal diet' followed by two weeks on a high carbohydrate diet, and another 24 hour lab row. The conclusion was that for an ocean row a high fat diet is preferable to the carbohydrate option. In 'technical' terms, the reason for this is the carbohydrate diet gives you a kind of wiz bang energy, good for sports requiring good energy levels for relatively short periods of time, but high fat gives a long slow burn better for the kind of situation the ocean rower is exposed to. A high fat diet is not recommended in 'normal' life even though it probably forms the basis if most people's diet in the western world, but when you are constantly exercising 12 hours out of 24 our sports science team reckoned the stats from the tests pointed in this direction. This would have been fine but much of the menu we ended up with on the boat was not really conducive to the environment in which we found ourselves and was often not particularly palatable. In short I would recommend food that is easy to prepare, just add water or boil in the bag type stuff. Food that is very nice to eat, anything that you doubt on land will become instantly chuckable once at sea. Lots of fresh fruit and veg to begin with, but it will soon go off so don't overdo it, and a good supply of treats and snacks. It is estimated that you will also consume about three times your 'normal' intake so this is worth bearing in mind. Emergency food and water should also be taken into consideration. Your food supplies will take up a large part of your boat's storage capability as well, so try and organise where you put everything so that you can gain access when you need it. A stowage plan is a good idea as after a few weeks at sea, or even a few days, you can easily forget where things are or even that you had them in the first place!

We had great nutrition from the perspective of the right amounts for each day's intake, to keep us going and not loose much weight, the problem was not a lot of thought had gone into combinations of food items and how they would be prepared. It's an area I learned a lot about in a short period of time and will improve a great deal upon the next time I go to sea.

Training provided the background to everything for two-and-a-half years. I enjoyed the challenge of it, although sometimes it became a bit onerous particularly time wise. It must be such a privilege to be a professional athlete and have the time and financial support to do the job properly, but, may be, if you are in that position it becomes just like any other job; I'll probably never know! Regarding injuries, I had occasional set backs but nothing hugely serious. The most constant problem was my right knee, which generally ached and on one occasion gave out, so I had to rest it for a few days. Apart from that I just got bigger and stronger and by the end of the programme felt well prepared for what lay ahead!

Chapter Nine

T he year 2000 saw the challenge enter a new phase regarding the boat, in so far as it was now time to fit her out for sea so that we could start sea trials. Whilst reflecting on some of the more academic elements of the project, I thought this would be a good opportunity to take a look at the costs involved in putting it all together. I compiled a comprehensive list for insurance purposes of almost everything we used. Boat equipment provides a good opportunity for 'sponsorship in kind', as companies will often be happy to donate a specific item of kit, especially if they manufacture or supply it. Failing that they may offer trade discounts which can represent considerable savings. If you are linked with a charitable cause this can also be an added incentive for a 'gift'. Every angle can help to lessen the financial impact on the project and a combination of strategies enabled me to achieve the best possible value for money.

So here is the list plus additional costs. I have not attempted to explain the use of individual items of gear as much of this has been covered in other chapters: -

Note: Listed items marked thus * were bought with cash, those marked ++ were donated as sponsorship in kind.

Boat Hull, Kit, labour and fittings	1	£10,000
Radar Reflector	1	£18.00*
Sea Anchor GP18L	1	£72.34*
Sea Brake Stowage Bag	1	£11.06*
Pur Watermaker 40E	1	£1995.00*
Spares Kit	1	£175.26*
Torch	2	£59.56*
Foghorn	1	£5.00*
Buckets	3	£13.38*
VHF Unit	1	£272.33*
Spare Battery	1	£45.60*
Waterproof Bag	1	£12.76*
Offshore Flares Pack+12 x white h'held		£202.60*
Fire blanket	1	£12.72*
Life jackets Commodore 160 NT Slim fit	2	£178.64*
Lifejacket lights	2	£20.00*

Lifejacket whistles	2	£4.00*
Lifejacket harnesses	2	£31.00*
Liferaft Lifeguard Forties 4 man + Atl Pk	1	£986.38++
Throwing line	1	£19.53*
Survival Suits and liners	2	£1000.00++

ORC Grab bag items

Second sea anchor	1	£56.00*
Signalling Mirror	1	£5.50*
Parachute Rocket Flares	2	£32.68*
Red Hand held flares	3	£16.65*
Bouyant smoke canister	1	£16.60*
Thermal protective aid	2	£17.00*
Solas No2 Card	1	£1.50*
Waterproof grab bag	1	£17.50*

Lights & Mast

Mast & all round white light	1	£65.00*
Cabin Lights	2	£30.00*

Compasses & Navigational Equipment

Plastimo Contest 130	1	£149.00*
Hand Bearing Compass	1	£70.00*
GPS Globalnav 212	2	£600.00++
GPS Globalnav 200	1	£250.00++
Charts	4	£150.00*
Sextant	1	£120.00*
Dividers	1	£15.00*
Plotter	1	£15.00*
Misc items pencils etc	various	£10.00*
Almanacs & tables	various	£100.00*

Ropes & Anchors

Parachute Anchor 9' Parachute	1	£350.00++
Mini Drouge	1	£50.00++
100mx12mm Para warp,bridle & fittings		£200.00++
Towing Warp 50mx10mm	1	£60.00++

Steering lines & fittings		£56.00++
Grablines 10mm		£20.00++
Spare lines & drogue warp		£25.00++

Cooking & Food

Sea Cook single burner stove	1	£120.00*
Food supplies for 90 days		£2000.00++
Water containers	17	£170.00*
Propane gas	60	£297.00*
Mini pressure cooker	1	£48.00*
Bowls and implements		£20.00++
Fishing Tackle		£30.00*

Oars & Seats

Sutton Oars	3 pairs	£1200.00*
Sliding Seats	4	£160.00*
Sheepskin & rubber pads		£42.00*
Rowing Gates,buttons and spares		£50.00*

EPIRB ACR Sat Cat 2 E12200	1	£446.81*
Mounting Bracket EPIRB	1	£31.06*
Anemometer	1	£70.00*
Barometer	1	£64.00*

Solar Rig

Fixed Panel	1	£800.00++
Flexible panel	1	£800.00++
Batteries	4	£250++
Controllers & wiring	2	£400.00++

Bilge pump fixed	1	£70.00*
Bilge pump portable	1	£20.00*

InmasatD+ Tracking system	1	£1000.00++
Palmtop HP Jornada	1	£398.00*
Leads		£7.00*

Toolkit	various items	£100.00++

Medical kit + additions		£400.00++
Clothing		
Foul Weather Gear	x2	£750.00++
Sun hats	2	£30.00++
Sun Glasses	x4	£100.00*
Clothing	various	£200.00++
Waterproof bags & containers	various	£100.00*
Sleeping bags	2	£40.00*

TOTAL: £27,847

The above list gives the full retail value of all items. For our entry we set up a company with the local Hospice, which we were fund raising for, and therefore benefited by being able to reclaim the 17.5% VAT on purchased items. However this meant that when the boat was sold it was liable for VAT, which had to be added to the sale price thus making it less competitive at that time. We also had trade accounts with various suppliers that enabled us to acquire discounts of over 50% in some cases. However, for the sake of the above I have reduced the total cost by 40% to give a very conservative idea of the real cost to us of the boat and equipment.

With this in mind, the total value of the exercise paying cash at retail prices is as above, i.e. **£27,847**. The value of items donated in kind came to **£10,347**, reducing that total to **£17,500**. This figure was then subject to a further reduction of 40% to cover re-claimed VAT and trade discounts on purchased items that gave a total cash figure of **£10,500**.

I included a total boat-building figure of **£10,000**. The boat kit cost **£2,350.00** and the rest of the materials were almost all donated. It took 500 man-hours to get the boat to basic build level, which enabled us to take her on the water and do training rows in sheltered conditions. I would estimate at least another 200 man-hours were taken to prepare her for sea. So the actual cost of the boat build, as we did it ourselves was probably around **£3,000**, including the price of the kit. So a further **£7,000** (representing a notional cost for our labour) could be subtracted from the **£10,500** figure, giving a final total of **£3,500**.

Additional Costs

Insurance:		£1,300
Flights:	Canary Is:	£400
	Barbados:	£800
Accommodation:	CI & Bar:	£2,000
Boat Shipment:	Out CI:	£2,000
	Trailer:	£600
	Back:	£2,200
Iridium Phone:	Set:	£500
	Calls:	£2,000
Challenge Business:	race fee:	£11,800
Tracking System:		£500
Gym & Training:		£4000
Total:		£28,100

So in total cash terms it probably cost us £28,100 plus £3,500 giving a total of £31,600.

In order to have done it from scratch with a budget at retail prices and little involvement from us as a crew, it would have cost around £56,000 *minimum*. However with time, huge commitment and a lot of hard graft and persuasion, we were able to reduce that figure to the £30-£35,000 mark in pure cash terms.

These costs are all at 2000 prices and obviously as time goes on percentage increases need to be considered. The actual challenge of achieving the final figure was an enjoyable task in itself but it is worthy of note to say, had we not had the time and strategy this would not have been possible. It also needs to be said that at the end of 2000, I was fortunate enough to have negotiated an open-ended interest free loan of £10,000 to cover all the outstanding costs at the time. Had this not been secured I am not sure where that extra funding would have come from, given the fact that time was running out. It was a bit of a gamble as I was only in a position to pay this back on the sale of the boat after the row. In the end I had a total debt of £15,000 after the project ended which I was able to clear through the sale of the boat some time after my return. Things could have been extremely bleak from a financial perspective if I had lost the boat at sea as no insurance cover for this eventuality was available at the time. You will become aware later in the narrative just how close I came to this scenario. Suffice to say, a book could be written purely on the financial experiences of ocean rowers, the highs of gaining sponsorship and the lows of managing the debts once the row is over. Like so many things in life, however, its all a bit of a gamble and provided you can manage the risk its well worth leaving the shore!

Chapter Ten

A pologies if the last two chapters were a bit tedious for those of you approaching the tale from the perspective of a good read. One of the problems with a writing project of this nature is where exactly to pitch it. Some people want the adventure aspects, others the human interest (often the angle the media will take), an individual pondering the prospect of an ocean row might like to have at least some idea of what they are letting themselves in for! I am attempting to give something for everyone, a strategy that the critics may not be too happy with but I don't really care, as I am not writing this for fame or fortune! In fact if that is your ambition I suggest an alternative sport to ocean rowing!

Anyway back to the plot. After reaching the 1999 deadlines, 2000 was a year of consolidation, PR, fundraising, endless training and assessments and the occasional high spot out on the water. A look at the diary shows the kind of things I got up to: for example, January 14th, Challenge Business, London Boat Show reception; February 3rd, Hospice Project management meeting (first of many), Feb 29th, BBC local radio interview (just one example of the many media opportunities throughout 2000), and March 4th, Chester for the initial bi-monthly fitness assessment peppering the five - six visits to the gym each week. I also did loads of summer fairs, various shows, a Business Breakfast Club meeting and numerous Hospice events.

The boat, meanwhile, was in the same basic state as she had been at the end of 1999. I was reluctant to do any sea trials until we had a full spec of safety equipment. This required a great deal of work as certain items, like a life raft, made to measure survival suits, flares and communications were targets for sponsorship in kind, partly because all our available funds were being channelled into keeping up to date with the regular Challenge Business quarterly payments. Cash flow was the real problem and it wasn't until I finally secured an interest free, open-ended loan of £10,000 in 2001 that we were able to complete our purchases and tackle the briny deep for the first time.

The level of activity increased with the arrival of 2001. I realised that I would need more time to pull everything together and negotiated a reduction in my contracted hours at work. My long-suffering employers agreed a cut from 37 hours to 30, which relieved the pressure a bit. The only problem with such a strategy is as soon as more hours theoretically become available they get filled. The New Year saw me setting out on a series of essential courses. The Challenge Business had recommended several, though I don't think they were compulsory, suffice to say it is probably a good idea to sign up for them especially if you are a real novice when it comes to the sea. There is a bit of a dilemma as to how near your departure you should do them as some of what you learn can be lost through the passage of time, especially if you don't normally use the knowledge you gain in your everyday life.

I had done 'O' Level Navigation at school, and almost got to pass my Able Seaman Certificate whilst at sea. I left a week before the exam which I will always regret as I would have passed easily. Many ocean sailing trips and a year 'before the mast' had given me a good grounding in matters maritime but all that was a long time ago. We had been told that one member of the rowing crew needed to have a good knowledge of navigation and should have done the RYA Ocean Yacht Masters Course (or at least the Astro Navigation element), plus VHF, first aid and sea survival courses. So these became the centre of my attention for the first few months of 2001. The astro nav course I found quite hard, I'm not the best at maths and I find bending my mind round spherical triangles and complicated correction tables a bit of a nightmare. When I was at sea, officers regularly made sun sights on a daily basis and I guess the repetition made the whole process second nature, but when you come to it cold after many years and don't use it all the time I am not entirely convinced of it's value for the modern day seafarer. For the ocean rower the vagaries of using a sextant and ten tons of nautical tables in a little boat that is pitching and rolling all over the place is questionable, especially when the result of your sight is probably within a few hundred miles of your real position - if you are lucky! The traditionalists would say you should not rely solely on GPS and other electronic gadgets, but even the Royal Navy class astro navigation as an emergency procedure, so I'm told, and those who know and understand the art are becoming few and far between with the passing years. Even the RYA, whilst insisting it remains a part of the syllabus for Ocean Yacht Master, regularly debate whether it should continue to be included, according to my navigation tutor. Having said that, it is a real art form and extremely satisfying if you can get it right and make it work for you. I think my feeling on the subject is it has probably reached it's sell by date, along with Morse Code, and it is more important to have a rudimentary grasp of general navigation, buoyage, metrology, sea state, seamanship, an intimate knowledge of how your GPS works and various survival strategies if all your electrics fail you. For instance it's helpful to know the sun rises in the east and sets in the west, and if your instruments fail on an east west Atlantic crossing, as long as you know how to keep going west you will eventually bump into some sort of land, even if it wasn't the destination you planned at the start!

I eventually took the Yacht Master exam, and just about passed, but I can't say I was enormously confident that I could find my way around with a sextant and pile of nautical tables. I was also a bit worried about sinking the boat when I finally amassed all the tables I would need! The three little hand held GPS units looked a much more realistic and manageable scenario, and, with the option of 'mains' or battery power and waterproof bags to stow them in, I reckoned this should see us through. The argument for astro navigation seems to be a stand by in case all else fails; my only problem with this is the premise seems to be that the sextant will never fail but GPS probably will, but what happens if the sextant gets broken or falls over the side, what about the tables getting ruined by sea water or the sun, moon or stars remaining obscured by cloud for days at a time? In the final analysis I don't think I will be bothering in future with the ancient art but I will carry my trusty sextant, if only to find my latitude in an emergency or my distance off the coast.

The other three courses were all one day affairs and not only informative and useful but also a good laugh. The Sea Survival course was conducted in the Worcester College for the Blind's swimming pool and involved a lot of swimming around in a survival suit (now in our possession thanks to a kind gift from BP, who supplied these made to measure along with our life raft). Rob came down for this one and we passed without incident. I did the VHF and First Aid on my own and again got through them having taken on board the necessary skills.

One of our sports science team had suggested I contact a Dr Mike Duke at South Bank University in London. He is an expert in solar power and builds the solar racing cars that race across Australia or the States annually. Mike was extremely interested in the project and glad to offer us his help and knowledge once I had been in touch and explained the challenge. After we had met a couple of times in London and discussed the project he came over to Worcester with a few students for a 'site visit'. They measured everything up and made loads of notes in order to design a suitable rig for the boat to supply all our power needs and build in a safety factor in case we had any problems. The South Bank team built the rig and tested it in London before making their way to install it at the beginning of April. The installation team had three Germans, five Koreans and Mike himself, a truly international gathering. They worked very hard on the boat fitting the panels, batteries, wiring and equipment. It was very cold and started snowing at one point which was a bit of a pain as the shed we had use of could only accommodate about two thirds of the boat length. Another visit was necessary before everyone was satisfied with the end result, which I have to say was absolutely fantastic. This was born out by a guy who turned up in Tenerife to inspect everyone's solar rigs and gave ours top marks. I'm no expert but I reckon ours was the best in the fleet! Mike and the team came down to Plymouth on the first day of our first sea trial to do further adjustments and test the system and two of his students came out to Tenerife before the start to do some final work for us. I was very touched by their dedication and enthusiasm for the project and the professionalism and expertise with which they set about the task.

Having mentioned the first sea trial I guess this would be a good time to add this to the tale! On May 25th. 2001, I borrowed a Range Rover and set off for Plymouth with Rob and our two nutritionists, Anna and Jose. Prior to leaving I had done a considerable amount of preparatory work deciding where our first trial would take place and the route we would adopt. For various reasons Plymouth seemed a good starting point and so I contacted the people at Queen's Anne's Battery Marina to ask if they would supply us with free launching and mooring for the weekend, having explained what we were doing. They declined but said there would be no problem for us to use the facilities at the usual rates. Same old story but by now we were used to the financial inconsistencies of the project. One minute someone who can't really afford it gives you an unexpected gift and the next minute you get a

Dr Mike Duke (left) and a team-member doing last minute checks before our first sea trial.

refusal from a business with plenty of dosh to spare even though they always claim poverty! However I guess it's a free country so you just have to grin and bear it.

We arrived in Plymouth about lunchtime on Friday and were met by our solar team who had come to make some final changes and adjustments. They worked on the boat whilst Anna and Jose packed the supplies they had organised for the menu over the next couple of days. After all the activity we retired to the Pub and then to my brother's place for a welcome evening meal. We retired to the boat to get some sleep before our departure on Saturday morning.

The original plan had been to row from Plymouth to Weymouth, but after some correspondence with the Coastguard and on the basis of the weather forecast we decided that this route would not be possible to achieve within the time and prevailing weather conditions. So we opted for plan B, which was to row over to Falmouth, and have my brother meet us there with the trailer. I had plotted our course, programmed the GPS and fairly early we slipped our moorings and headed out of the marina on our way to open water. It was a slightly odd feeling as the last time I rowed a boat in this part of the world was 25 years earlier as a Merchant Navy Cadet taking my lifeboat coxswain's certificate as part of my training at Plymouth School of Maritime Studies. That was, however, a long time ago and the place looked very different from when it was dominated by the Seamanship School.

We headed for the Eastern Channel side of the Breakwater. The weather the previous day had been very windy and wet with a lot of fog, not good if it persisted. By morning there was still a lot of mist about but the weather forecast was good and the promise of a fine day lay ahead. I guess fog was one of the things I wanted to avoid on this, our first sea passage, and wind on a lee shore was the other scenario that could have caused some consternation. If the weather overpowers you in one of these boats there comes a point when you really can't do anything, particularly if the wind is stronger than your pulling power, apart from deploying a drogue or Para Anchor, or using a conventional anchor if you are close inshore, the water is not too deep and there isn't any breaking surf. It is said that the most hazardous points of an ocean row are the first and last 100 miles when a land mass can become a problem, but taking the weather, currents and tides into account and making the right decisions should make for a safe passage.

Once we had arrived in the vicinity of the breakwater and were heading out into the Sound, a short, steep, sea kicked in resulting from opposing wind and tide. It was

The author rowing out into Plymouth Sound.

the first time we had really encountered such conditions and there was a little anxiety regarding how the boat would perform.

I had taken the first rowing shift, we having planned a two hourly rotation. I had asked Rob to go into the cabin and check the function of the GPS, as the idea of this trip was to test every aspect of the boat gear and ourselves as was possible in such a short time frame. In hindsight this was a mistake as once the motion had picked up in the entrance to the Eastern Channel, Rob found it too much and came out of the cabin looking very green. He was soon in a poor state through seasickness, constantly throwing up a variety of multi coloured offerings, most over the side but some on deck. We headed on out. I had planned to row in the direction of the West Tinker Buoy and then set a course for the Eddystone Lighthouse. At a way point some way short of the light we would turn West for Falmouth. I rowed on to complete my two hours, the sea had become more benign with a long rolling swell, what was left of the fog had burnt off and the sun came out. For once we had a beautiful day to accompany us. Unfortunately, though, Rob was in no state to appreciate it and I asked him if he wanted to take his turn at the oars. He was keen to do so, probably to give his mind something else to concentrate on. He duly took over and I repaired to the cabin for some food. It was decided to head back for Plymouth as the prospect of Rob's state continuing and me having to row constantly until we got to Falmouth was not a sensible course of action. In the meantime I had some of the food we had been given for the trip. As I said before I think there was a lot to have been desired regarding the substance of our menu for the actual trip when it took place later in the year, but to be honest the same applied to what was on offer that weekend. I guess there were certain things the sea trial threw up (if you'll pardon the pun!) that I hadn't given enough attention to or perhaps even ignored. A friend of mine later summed up the reason for this. He reckons that risk takers can have a certain amount of tunnel vision; we set our focus on the goal and the deadlines that have to be met to achieve that end result. This can be a great advantage because it gets the job done, no matter what the obstacles; conversely it can also cause you to ignore clear warning signs that may eventually seriously compromise your ability to succeed in reaching your goal, or at worst cause you to fail completely. Balancing these two problems can probably only come through experience or the services of a good mentor who is not afraid to challenge your thinking or actions, and to be honest a large dollop of good fortune.

We headed back in past the breakwater and for the final part of the return journey, took up the oars together. Once inside the harbour Rob's state improved and we eventually arrived back at QAB. We informed the team of developments and that I was determined to go out again the next day to try and help Rob get over his fairly negative experience.

The next morning we headed out again, moored on the inside of the breakwater and had some food, then took a row around the area testing the watermaker and electrical system for the first time. I then took the boat into the breaking waves at the entrance to the Eastern Channel, again with the breakwater on our starboard beam. I spent a very enjoyable period surfing the boat up and down in this area, testing her and gaining confidence all the time. Rob remained in the cabin during this time and managed not to succumb to further seasickness. As a result I felt the two days had been partially successful and had certainly enabled us to test equipment previously unused.

In hindsight, however, we should have both been a bit more objective about our experience and taken action, within the ever-decreasing count down to the start of the race, to address the conclusions, which may have helped us not to have ended up with a less than satisfactory final outcome. Having said that it wasn't only Rob and food that would finally shatter the dream, a number of other contributing factors were waiting just over the horizon.

Chapter Eleven

There was no let up in the pace of things on my return from Plymouth. The following Saturday I was due to take the boat to Ombersley, a village just outside Worcester where my local Q-Guild butcher has his shop. Checketts is a family business that has been going for 100 years. One of the brothers who run the business had suffered the tragic loss of a son through cancer and had consequently had a great deal to do with St Richard's Hospice. They had helped me with some sponsorship and had developed a special sausage 'The Atlantic Voyager' to add to their prize winning varieties, 10p of each pound purchased going direct to the Hospice. They also make their own Biltong, a delicacy originating from South Africa comprising of meat dried with spices into chewy strips, which are a good source of protein and an excellent snack for ocean rowers. They provided me with 100 vacuum packed portions of this excellent product for the trip. Anyway on Saturday, June 2nd, they had publicised a barbeque event outside the shop and the tables, chairs, parasols and copious amounts of food and drink set the boat off very well. It was a great day and raised a considerable sum for the work of the Hospice.

The next day I towed the boat up to the Hospice for a Volunteers Day. This was an opportunity for the organisation to say thanks to its many volunteers and the boat and Atlantic Challenge took centre stage.

Broadway was my destination the following Saturday. This quintessential Cotswold village lies on the edge of the county, about 25 miles from Worcester, and I had been invited to display the boat at a two day Garden Party in aid of the Hospice. It all went very well, even though I found myself answering the same old questions I had been asked at countless events over many months. When you feel so committed to a project though, it is a pleasure to talk about it even if you do cover the same old ground rather a lot!

On June 27th, the Challenge Business had asked us if we would be happy to take the boat down to Southampton to do a PR shoot with Ward Evans, the race sponsors. We were happy to oblige and arrived at a hotel just outside Southampton the night before where we met a couple called Debra and Andrew Veal. They had entered the race but had no boat at the time so were to row the old prototype owned by the CB.

The following day we made for the port and met everyone involved. We rowed well out into Southampton Water and the Veals were towed out by the photographer's rib. We rowed around a big tanker that dwarfed our little boats but made a dramatic background for the pictures. After a couple of hours we were towed back whilst the other two rowed. After a pleasant lunch at the marina we packed up and headed back to the slipway where we retrieved the boat and left for home.

The following Sunday was our debut on national TV, the BBC having contacted me some weeks before. I thought this was our big break, a TV contract to appear on an extreme sports programme and gain national exposure. After all we had managed it with a two page article in the national 'Men's Health' magazine about a year before, so I guess this looked like a natural progression. In fact it turned out to be 'Songs of Praise'! Apparently they had recorded two programmes at Worcester Cathedral and were looking for local interest stories to go between the hymns. It transpired they had done a piece on a patient at the Hospice and found out about us. They thought it would be good to add this to the mix! Ah well, it's all good experience and of benefit to the Hospice so we spent the day on the river with the film crew and Pam Rhodes. Well Pam actually turned up for the interview and we did the rest. It all went very well and the following day found me at the Hospice doing some extra shots with some of the patients. In fact the end result was very good and made a nice piece to pop into our media portfolio. In case you were wondering, however, no, they didn't sing 'For those in peril on the sea'!

The year raced on. In July, Usha, Josh, John and I headed north, so John and I could do the Coast to Coast cycle route. I think it's about 130 miles from Whitehaven to Sunderland, across the Lake District and Pennines. It was a great adventure for us both and good to spend time with John. The scenery was fantastic as was the weather. The only major mishap that could have been a potential disaster was on the third day, when I came flying down a hill with a bend at the bottom. As usual John had gone off ahead; being light, agile and fit he always whizzed up the hills whilst muscle bound me pedalled on slowly but surely in his wake. I had the advantage of my own personal secret weapon on the downhill sections as my extra weight surrendered to the earth's gravitational pull! The turbo effect was operating as I came round the corner, not expecting anything to be coming in the opposite direction. I was on the wrong side of the road in order to gain the maximum momentum up the next hill. To my horror a Land Rover was heading straight for me, my life flashed before me (well almost) as I realised that I was going to fast to try and get back onto the other side of the road; if I had, the bike would have gone from under me and I would have ended up under the vehicle either dead or in need of a service (possibly religious)! The other option would have been to keep my present course, but this would have meant hitting the bull bar and probably ending up flying over the roof breaking every bone in my body on the way. I suddenly realised there was one more option and that was to try and aim the bike through the narrow gap between the Land Rover and the dry stone wall on the passenger side. This was a risky strategy as there really wasn't much room but the grassy bank looked better than the tarmac or bull bar so I headed for the gap. Everything was a blur, somehow I missed the wall and the bike came crashing down on the road just behind the back of the vehicle, which by this time had stopped and disgorged its husband and wife occupants who raced to my aid as I lay on the road covered in grass! I was a bit shaken and rather embarrassed, apologising profusely to the shocked looking couple. They were very understanding, almost apologetic which is a bit of a laugh considering it was entirely my fault. Once they ascertained I was in one piece they went on their way and I caught up with John who by this time was beginning to wonder if something had happened. We completed the route on day four with a great sense of satisfaction and a warm feeling of achievement.

We came back on Thursday, July 26th, and on the Saturday I took the boat to the Mayor's Garden Party in Pershore. It was yet another Hospice do at which some bloke in a kilt tried to teach me to play the bagpipes…don't ask! I was presented with two medals commemorating a landmark in Pershore's history. The idea was to take them with us and perhaps auction them on our return as a fundraiser.

Time was moving so fast and on Saturday, September 8th, Rob came to help pack the boat with all the food and equipment we would need ready to take her down to Felixstowe to be shipped to Tenerife. On Sunday we had an official farewell do at Cannons Health Club, even though we were not due to depart for another couple of weeks. We finished everything on the Monday and set out early on September 11th for Felixstowe. After an uneventful trip to the port we found the container depot and left the boat and trailer in the hands of the shipping company. This was a big emotional step as it was the first time the boat had been trusted to someone else, someone who had no regard for the years of time and effort we had invested in her. There were a few other boats there and we looked over these with interest before heading home. On arrival my son John came rushing out and said "Hey Dad, come and have a look at this!" I followed him into the lounge and was shocked to see the images on TV. It all seemed a bit unreal, as I saw the planes fly into the Twin Towers of the World Trade Centre in New York. We had been oblivious to this horrific event all day but now there it was, right before me. I wondered if this would affect the race but hoped it would not.

On Tuesday, September 18th, I had to attend a government seminar in Birmingham and whilst there visited one the of biggest computer shops in the area. This was all part of the ongoing saga of Inmarsat D+, the Challenge Business's compulsory tracking system with a recommended add on, comprising a palm top computer which would send simple text messages to and from the boat, providing a basic communications system to crews who, for one reason or another (mainly financial), choose not to invest in a satellite telephone system. A couple of weeks before departure I wanted to make sure that I had everything necessary to enable this system to work. I had been in touch with World Cruising Club, part of the Challenge Business, which was responsible for the system. The instructions we were sent told us that we would need a lead with an RS232 connection for the two devices to talk to each other, i.e. the Inmarsat D+ unit and Palm Top. I tried in vain to acquire this item in all the Worcester computer shops, however, and talked to a guy called James Hall who said I would need a 'null modem serial cable' or something. I went everywhere with the exact specification James had told me, written on a piece of paper, but none of the shops had any idea of what was required and hence the Birmingham shop. I thought that one of the biggest computer suppliers in the city is bound to know what I was on about. Once again, however, I was met with all sorts of suggestions, none of which would have done the trick. I thought the best thing to do was get James on my mobile and give it to the manager so he could explain exactly what I needed. The ensuing conversation drew a blank and by now I was getting pretty frustrated with only days to go to our departure and our only means of communication with the outside world looking in doubt because of a piece of cable. When I got home I rang James again and he decided the best tactic would be for me to go to a website he identified and order it on the net, he even gave me the part number. I logged on and found after a long search that no such part existed! This was getting ridiculous! I called James back knowing I only had days and beginning to doubt whether there would be time to get it delivered if this elusive item did exist at all. He was very apologetic and gave me another website and part number and this time I actually found and duly ordered it. It cost me £24 with all the postage and packing, the part itself was less than a pound!

Our solar team had installed the unit for us but we had been told by the CB that their engineer Keith Baxter would be on hand in Tenerife to install units for teams who hadn't had anyone with the expertise to do it and in order to check those that had. So we left with the confidence that we would have the necessary means to communicate and someone out in the Canaries to ensure it was working. However during this final frantic phase before departure, and as a result of my conversations with James Hall, I found out that the number of characters we could send on this system was far less than we had been previously told and that the costs would be relatively high. This had the effect of seriously compromising our media strategy. I had also been informed that I needed to appoint someone at home to act as a contact person and that World Cruising would need to know who this was and have a base email address. None of this had been communicated prior to departure; this information had not been made clear within any of the pre race meetings. Probably just as well, then, that I had this dialogue with World Cruising prior to departure. The reason for explaining this at some length is because the problems we experienced with this communications package played a central role in what was to happen once we were at sea. We were not the only ones to suffer from the failure of this system to perform, as you will see later.

At last the day arrived for us to leave for Tenerife, Tuesday, September 25th, dawned and we had arranged for Chris Spears to take Usha, Josh and I to Birmingham Airport, where we were due to meet Rob and his family for the flight out. My daughter Nayna had a geography field trip and had only just started university, so she would not be joining us, but John was due to fly out on his own for the start of the race as his school would not let him have the time off.

We flew out on a charter flight, one of these efforts where you have to have your legs amputated to fit in the seat. Once you have been surgically implanted in it you can't really move, which probably means you will die of a blood clot once you have reached your destination, even if they manage to sew your legs back on successfully. Of course you also have to pay for everything on the plane, which is another down side of these charter efforts, so if you have forgotten your cash or not brought anything with you, you may well expire from dehydration as well! To be honest the only thing going for them is that they are cheap; everything else about travelling on a charter flight is, in my opinion, a thoroughly unpleasant experience!

We had arranged a couple of hire cars at the airport in Tenerife and picked them up without any problem. It was about 0200 hours when we headed off in the direction of Los Gigantes, where we had rented a villa for two weeks prior to the start of the race that was scheduled to take place a short walk down the road at the marina. We found the place with some difficulty, as there was no one to ask at three in the morning! Some doubt had been cast on whether or not the start would take place from the marina, prior to our departure, by some conversations I had had with a guy called Kenneth Crutchlow who had directed me to read a press article, taken from a Tenerife newspaper, which stated that the Harbour Master at Los Gigantes would not allow the start to take place from there. I considered this to be mere speculation, however, as I had not heard anything to that effect from the organisers and was sure they had made all the necessary arrangements, as we had been consistently told from when we registered in 1998 that it would start from there.

Talking of Kenneth Crutchlow it would be a good moment to introduce this larger than life figure. I had met him and his wife, Tatiana, at Jan Meek's presentation a couple of year's before but had obviously not really registered this fact until Tatiana showed me a photo of us at this function after my return. It was only fairly close to the race date that the CB issued information about their logistics package. The problem was that it originally came in at about £7,500, causing a bit of dissention amongst most teams. In fact at the last team meeting in London, which was the only one Rob and I had been unable to attend, logistics was the main item on the agenda, or so I was informed. By all accounts there was a little unease at the price of this package and as the result of some lively dialogue about £1,000 was lopped off the top of this. At this stage in the proceedings, with most teams struggling with the financial burden of the challenge, £6,500 represented a very large commitment, money that most of us still had to find. Kenneth Crutchlow heads up the Ocean Rowing Society, an organisation that has served the interests of ocean rowers for nearly 21 years. Up until a few months before the race I had never heard of the ORS or Kenneth, but he was offering a much cheaper package of around £4,500 to competitors. I was a bit wary of this to begin with as we had dealt with the CB for the last 3 years and suddenly this guy appears on the scene, who I had never heard of and with no track record so far as I was concerned. I asked Teresa Evans for her opinion of this offer but she was very non-committal. As the package was financially very attractive relative to the CB I thought it worth pursuing. I wrote to Kenneth, asking him for all intents and purposes to sell me his package and convince me that it was worthy of pursuit, as I didn't want to end up with egg on my face having invested so much in the project to date. In hindsight I was probably a bit hard on him and certainly ignorant of his background, which was a shame as his commitment to ocean rowing is second to none, but I have learnt that Kenneth has very broad shoulders and will always go the extra mile for those who wish to row the oceans. At the time, however, and under the circumstances I think my reservations were understandable. Once I thought we should adopt the ORS package and began to have more frequent conversations with Kenneth I warmed to him, particularly as he seemed to know what he was on about. As it transpired, just about the whole fleet ended up in Kenneth's care and he did a magnificent job sorting out all the logistics for the whole race at sensible rates.

So we finally arrived in Tenerife and after a bit of sleep registered for the race. We were staying next door to the club where the CB had set up their HQ, which was very handy. We registered and made our way to Playa San Juan. San Juan is a little fishing port about six miles to the South of Los Gigantes, where the boats were delivered prior to the fleet moving North to Los Gigantes three days before the start. We were told they would be located in a secure guarded area on the breakwater where teams could work on the boats and train in the couple of weeks still remaining. The security was a joke to be frank, I think there was some sort of guard but to this day I am still not sure if this was an official arrangement or just the normal guy on the dock gates as he certainly didn't seem bothered who gained access. There was no secure area for the boats and with each one fully equipped and worth anything upwards of £30,000 this scenario was less than satisfactory to put it mildly! So with a couple of weeks until the race start we set about our final preparations hoping the boat would be safe and our gear wouldn't get nicked.

Our first visit to Playa San Juan, to see if our boat was still in one piece.

Chapter Twelve

T he Challenge Business was arranging boat inspections on all boats over the next two weeks and we arranged for ours to be done the next day, giving us plenty of time to make any changes that may have been necessary. We set off early on Thursday, September 27th, to arrive at San Juan at about 0800 hours for the inspection. There were a number of CB staff around and two of them set to work on the boat. We were checked against a standard list and everything appeared to be in order, apart from an extra u bolt which we were asked to fit to the bulkhead in the well fore of the cabin hatch as an additional point to secure our lifelines when in that area or entering and leaving the cabin. It was sound advice although most teams found it quite hard to get parts in the area, and when they did they were pretty expensive. During the morning Keith, the electrical engineer, came to see us. He said he understood we had the right parts for the Inmarsat D+ two-way messaging system although there had already been a lot of debate between him and James at World Cruising about whether or not the cable was correct or necessary. This was a bit worrying as they didn't really seem to be sure of exactly how the whole system should be enabled to work properly. Keith asked if he could borrow the lead and connectors and would we mind if he cut it and changed the configuration of the wires inside in order to get everyone's system working. As he seemed to know what he was up to I agreed but insisted that he returned it and made sure our system was in full operational order before he left.

We then had a series of meetings, either at the Oasis Club next door to our villa or in the Hotel Los Gigantes, just around the corner. The first of these was on Sunday 30th and gave an update on various aspects of the race. One item raised was the lack of a power and water supply in San Juan that had made it difficult for teams to work on their boats. We were told the CB would try and sort something out.

The lack of security, power and water supply were not the only things that made life difficult for us. The only launching facilities were provided by 'El Craneo'. El Craneo, as we 'lovingly' christened him, was the guy who operated the crane on the dock normally reserved for unloading fishing boats. He would appear in the morning and then disappear for one of those long Spanish lunch breaks, lasting from about 1200-1500 hours, so if you launched and weren't back at the right time a long wait would ensue. The other problem was the charges, it was about £7 for each launch and retrieval, and whilst there was the alternative of a slipway no provision had been made for a vehicle to facilitate this. The majority of crews were strapped for cash and whilst the fee may seem not that expensive it just added one more item to the long list of additional charges we found ourselves having to pay. This wouldn't have been so bad if El Craneo had given us value for money. The fact is that he was less than conscientious when working the boats and his lack of regard ended up with at least two being holed when they were dropped on their trailers. With more planning and foresight a vehicle with a tow bar could have been hired for team use or the CB could have arranged to hire the crane for the period with their own operator.

Throughout the build up to the start of the race, work on the boats, safety checks and the occasional race briefing continued including use of the first aid kit and weather. On Monday, October 1st, the calendar of events stated, 'Last day for installation of Inmarsat D+ units'. Keith was about to fly back to the UK and there had been no sign of the return of our lead. I was a little worried about this, as not only had it not been returned but also no work had been done on our boat as promised to make sure that the messaging was working, even though the tracking system had been checked. I was assured that the cable would make the system work and it would be left in the boat cabin before he went. Well sure enough it was and we plugged it in to test it. The Palm Top didn't appear to be sending messages and so towards the end of the week I managed to get one of the CB staff to check it with his lap top computer. He assured me that it was working, although I was not so sure. Because everyone was rushed off their feet there really wasn't any more time for the CB to check the system properly at both ends, send test messages and make sure the whole system was functional for all the teams using it.

Prior to the start we had a free day and decided to drive into the interior of the island. The Canaries are entirely volcanic and El Tiede is the volcano that marks the highest point on the island. The coastal regions of Tenerife have been wrecked by tourism in an attempt to capitalise on the provision of cheap package holidays. Huge sprawling developments designed to pack in as many punters as possible and relieve them of their hard earned cash appears to be the basis of planning philosophy. However, if you take time to get away from all of this you will be greatly rewarded. The trip up to El Tiede is stunning with fantastic views and what can only be described as a lunar landscape, as you wind your way round some challenging mountain roads that often seem to be holding on to the mountainside by their finger nails. You go through pine forest and over solidified lava flows and the final few miles to the top are quite magical, with the strange natural sculptures left by the violence of previous volcanic activity. It was a really good day out and nice to get away from the race preparations for a short while. As we descended from the heights of El Tiede I remember looking down on the black mass of La Gomera, the next island out in the Canary group as the setting sun reflected like burnished gold on the vast expanse of the Atlantic Ocean, knowing it would not be long now before we would be heading out past the island and ever onward to the vast horizon that shone before us.

During the pre race period various people from Ward Evans, the race sponsors, had appeared along with their PR company representatives. Large banners started to appear around Los Gigantes, announcing the race and its start on October 7th. Rumours had been rife that an ongoing dispute between the Los Gigantes Harbour Master and the CB had resulted in the race start being banned from the Los Gigantes Marina. Unfortunately no clear direction was given to the teams as to whether or not the race would eventually start from there. The idea had been for all the teams to row up from San Juan three days before the start and moor in the marina for final preparations. CB staff constantly told us that they were working on a solution to the problem and at our last briefing session all sorts of compromises were suggested, as it was clear by this stage the Los Gigantes Marina start was not going to happen. The alternative seemed to be for the start to be moved to San Juan. However this caused real problems for everyone as guests, family and friends had been told the race would start from Los Gigantes. Any decision to change this had been left too late for many people to be informed and make alternative arrangements. The race sponsors had invested several thousand pounds in publicity materials for a Los Gigantes start so a change would also scupper their PR strategy. The suggested compromise was for the race to start off the breakwater at San Juan and for all of us to row the six miles up the coast to a marker buoy just off the Los Gigantes Marina. Each team would round the buoy and their crossing time would be started at this point, guests, sponsors and supporters watching from the marina breakwater. Needless to say most of us were pretty unhappy about this state of affairs, as this only became the official position of the organisers less than 48 hours before the start. It was never made clear why the failure to deliver this happened, and I am not about to speculate, but it did represent an almighty cock up.

This meant we had to launch our boats the night before the race and moor them on buoys in the harbour at San Juan. On the basis that we should have been moored on a pontoon at Los Gigantes by this time, we asked for the CB to arrange a free lift for each team into the water at San Juan, but one CB representative made the comment in response to this entirely reasonable request "****** don't you know how much this is costing us?!" The fact that we had paid a huge sum of money to participate seemed irrelevant and I am afraid this kind of response appeared to underpin much of our dealings with the organisers. All the requests teams made at gatherings in the run up to the start where entirely reasonable, even if they may have had a tiny effect on profit margins.

In the end some arrangement was made for a lorry with a tow bar to come and launch the boats. This was masterminded by a local guy who ultimately relieved a few teams of their trailers. By this time of course the teams in question were at sea and it was only after their return that they became aware that their trailers had been stolen.

At long last Sunday, October 7th, arrived and with it the start of the race. At this point I think I will turn to my diary account of what happened as it was written at the end of the first week on the island of El Hierro. Why there? Read on and find out!

Well here we are in La Restinga on the island of El Hierro, ok I know, it´s time to get the world Atlas out and find out where it is. Suffice to say, if you visit the lighthouse down the coast from here, they will award you with a certificate saying you have visited 'the World´s End´!

I should be about 300 miles out into the Atlantic today but instead I´m stuck here in La Restinga trying to sort out communications equipment so I can continue on to Barbados, as a participant but no longer a competitor in the Ward Evans Atlantic Rowing Challenge.

The days since the start have been a complete roller coaster of emotion, physical exhaustion, mental anguish and continuous toil and hard work, there have been some good bits too!!

So here is a potted history of the whole adventure to date.

The start day, Sunday, October 7th, dawned, I just didn´t realise how hard it would be to say goodbye to Usha, Joshua, John, Rob´s family and Barney, Ann, Jeannie and Rob who had come out from St Richard´s.

The race start had been rife with controversy as to where it would be. In the end it was from Playa San Juan not Los Gigantes even though one team had rowed up there and wondered where everyone else was! We were told the final decision was made to leave from San Juan rather than row the six miles up the coast to Los Gigantes, round a buoy and head out into the Atlantic, (the organisers compromise to race sponsors and supporters for their inability to organise the start they had always maintained would be from Los Gigantes) as there was bad weather forecast, which sounded a bit ominous!

 All 36 teams headed out into the Atlantic full of hope. All, except those who could not get their boats launched in time and were left behind at the start. Rob and I rowed together for about an hour during which time the fleet dispersed and disappeared from view leaving us alone. He took the first solo shift and so began our sea going race routine. As we were passing Gomera a ferry hove in view which I soon ascertained was approaching on a constant bearing, for any of you who aren't old sea dogs, a vessel approaching another on a constant bearing means that sooner or later as your respective courses converge a collision will ensue if no avoiding action is taken! Large ferry + small rowing boat = disaster, so out came a white anti collision flare in case they ignored us or didn't even see us in the first place. In the end they did see us but didn't alter course and I only just had time to turn the boat bows up to counter the rather large bow wave that could have capsized us.

Fond farewells: Rob & the author wave goodbye as they are taken out to their boat.

Final checks on board.

And we're off!

By this time the weather was deteriorating and the seas mounting. Rob had managed to stave off the seasickness but wasn't looking very happy with life. Apart from the rowing shifts he stayed in the cabin without a word. If you know him as well as I do this is quite out of character. The conditions got worse and finally we were rowing in a near gale situation I would estimate 12-15 foot waves some of which had breaking crests. However the boat behaved magnificently for which I am very grateful and most impressed, it is a great design.

This weather continued for about 3 days, we hadn't eaten much and by now were both absolutely exhausted, not just the kind of tiredness you feel at the end of the day but an all pervading exhaustion from lack of food, sleep, and constant physical effort. This was not just from the rowing but just having to hang on and do energy sapping jobs like deploying our parachute anchor which keeps the bows of the boat into the weather and stops you going broadside on to the sea.

On day two we had a passing visit from Challenge 47 one of the two safety yachts following the race. I saw her mast some way off and hailed her on the VHF. I took this action because by then I had doubts that the satellite text messaging system we had on board was functioning properly. This was a key safety feature as well as a way of communicating with people back at home. We had been given coded single letter or number messages (e.g. 2 = I am taking on water and require immediate assistance). We had a chat with the electrician on board and sent a test message. They then left saying they would be back later in the day to confirm it was working. They never returned.

After the weather calmed down a bit both of us, now completely drained discussed the situation Rob very definitely wanted to pull the plug he just couldn't face going on. In deference to him I sent a message saying we wished to retire, as this is really the only course of action if one or other rower wants to leave the boat. I asked for assistance via the text service and we settled down to wait for the yacht. By now the weather had greatly improved and I got up early to row at may be 0400, it was great and I felt much better because now we were progressing in the right direction. I still hadn't given up hope of continuing but realised that Rob's condition was improving fast with the thought of leaving the boat and heading for home. When the yacht arrived Rob could leave and I could press on alone.

After two days scanning an empty horizon I realised that the messaging service probably wasn't working as I had previously suspected. Not trying to do to much finger pointing but this was really as a result of problems I had had with World Cruising who manage the system plus connecting and testing the system with Challenge Business staff in Tenerife before we left.

It was now becoming a matter of safety and with the last island of the Canary chain still in sight albeit some 40 nm away against the wind we made a decision to row 1 hour on 1 hour off for the 24 hours or so it would take us to reach safety. This we did and arrived in Peurto La Estaca about midday on Saturday. We had no money, no means of communication and felt pretty isolated. Eventually we managed to change a bit of cash Rob had and with some local help from the inhabitants of El Hierro I was able to ring home. It was a very emotional call, after 3.5 years of planning, training, fundraising and sheer hard work, here I was out of the race not knowing quite what to do, particularly as I hadn't had the chance to talk the Challenge Business and come up with an informed choice of any options still left open to us!

Rowing towards El Hierro and the end of the dream?

The reason for this was primarily because we had been given two 'emergency' contact points by the CB one was a pager number and the other a phone number. Neither resulted in a response and to add insult to injury the telephone number had an answer phone message telling us the office was closed over the weekend! I suppose it would have been unreasonable to expect the organisers of a major international sporting challenge for which individual teams had paid thousands of pounds to participate, to have been available on their own emergency contact numbers at the weekend! The problem for Rob and I was the fact that we had very little money available and the pay phone was eating that up fast. In the end my wife contacted the Ocean Rowing Society and she was given the race organisers mobile number. This number had never been issued to us prior to the start and was the reason why we were left stranded for a considerable time. In fairness to Teresa Evans whose number it was, when contact was eventually made she did apologise profusely for the problems we had had.

Anyway thanks to my absolutely brilliant wife Usha, who has become the real star of this whole project, I got a call from Teresa Evans CB Project Manager. She informed me that it would be OK to continue single handed if I so wished and she had asked Challenge 47 to divert and meet us at Estaca then tow us to La Restinga at the other end of El Hierro whilst effecting repairs to the text service. They eventually arrived in the evening and invited us on board over night. We departed for La Restinga 10 miles up the coast about 0900 on Sunday with the 'Spirit of Worcestershire' in tow. The guy from the yacht worked on the text messaging all morning but seemed unable to get it going and the guy he needed to speak to at World Cruising had gone sailing and could not be reached, (probably a bit like the CB HQ number not being manned at the weekend!) We arrived off La Restinga in the afternoon but the yacht could not enter the little port for fear of it being to shallow. They had to leave to assist another boat so we rowed in to yet another strange port even more isolated than the last. We moored up and found ourselves once again strangers in a foreign land without cash and still no communications!!!!

Anyway we were shortly introduced to 'The English Lady` as the locals who were happy to assist us knew her. Babette Moreau is an incredible person who has adopted us for these few days and done a huge amount to make us welcome and help us out. She is one of the few people on this isolated island that has internet access and also offered us the use of her phone.

Communications restored, Usha and a number of others back in the UK managed to secure a satellite phone that is on its way as I write. My intention is to attempt a single-handed crossing provided the window of opportunity remains open which probably gives me until Wednesday. The only down side to this strategy is it could take me 90 days so apologies in advance to my employers!

Why am I going on? Its not soon enough to throw in the towel, I committed myself to this project for many years, I wanted it to be something that would inspire others to be involved in and give. Many have given their time, energy, skills and finance and whilst I know they feel I have already given it my best shot, there is still powder in the barrel. We still have great opportunities to focus the row in giving to the work of St Richard´s and now more than ever, I am appealing to everyone in South Worcestershire to give your support and throw your cash at the Hospice.

The author discusses his options with Babette.

Now I must prepare myself and the boat to face what will, I´m sure, be the ultimate challenge.

Richard Wood
October 16[th,] 2001

This was the raw text from the diary entry that I wrote from La Restinga. It is pretty matter of fact, however, so before I leave this chapter I would like to fill in a few details. First of all the weather. Within the great plan of things the weather we encountered in the first few days was not extreme, I have experienced far worse, with waves of 60 feet not 12, but suffice it to say I was in a large general cargo ship at the time! In comparison with the conditions other ocean rowers have experienced over the years this was not extreme. However, for the first time out on the pond in such a small boat it can be a bit of a shock, particularly if you have never been to sea before for any length of time. So it is hard to know beforehand how each individual will react or respond in such an environment. You may have noted that we used the Para Anchor on a couple of occasions? This wasn't entirely necessary but when deployed it performed magnificently, giving us some respite that under the circumstances was necessary, particularly with the way Rob was feeling. Rob's condition was hard to understand and I will put his response to it into the text a bit later for you to draw your own conclusions. All I can say is after over 20 years of friendship and sometimes in testing circumstances when we both had to rely on each other, the way he responded was perplexing. For example on previous trips we had done on mountain bikes or kayaking he would always be the first to get out the cooking gear at the end of the day and make a meal or a brew to revitalise us. He would often be out ahead when on a trip and would be waiting for me to catch up at our destination! This was a scenario we were both happy with although it wasn't really something we discussed, it was just one of those givens that become an accepted part of getting to know each other well over a long period of time. So when he just shut down, which is the only way I can describe it, suddenly the bloke you had known all those years and the mutual reliance on each other ceased to exist. He did continue to do his two hour rowing shift but very little else and his mind seemed to be elsewhere, perhaps back at home with his family. The sea does strange things to people and anyone entering a challenge like this without a large helping of respect can only be described as foolish. My personal philosophy of the mighty oceans is to treat them with *great* respect and pray they will allow you to reach the other side in one piece, or at least return in that state. Nothing is given and if the weather gets up, you hit a disaster or your mind packs up, you won't be the first to try and weather the storm; the outcome may be unpredictable and even beyond your control. It could lead to a personal encounter with your maker so it is best to be well prepared before you leave for any such scenario!

When we did finally confront the situation and talk about it there didn't really seem any alternative under the circumstances other than to seek assistance, so Rob could leave the boat. I will say more about this later but if the yacht had come when required the outcome for me could have been very different. I cannot really explain the immediate change in Rob once the decision had been made and we eventually started the row back to El Hierro. Suddenly the old Rob returned, it was like switching on a light. This was particularly hard for me, especially once we had arrived on the island as Rob's clear delight at talking to his wife and the prospect of going home was something I couldn't share, as all I wanted to do was get on with the challenge.

Having said that Rob was a great partner for the run up to the race and did a great job with the boat building which, although a shared responsibility, fell more on his shoulders in so far as she was built just up the road from his house and 200 miles from mine! We had a great deal of fun in the three-and-a-half-years of preparation and met a lot of wonderful people, so I look back on that with little or no regret.

Perhaps at this stage I should hand over the text to Rob's diary entry which he wrote after the return from El Hierro, to inform supporters of how he felt. It is perhaps an interesting insight on how the row affected one person and should be treated with respect as we are all different and a project of this nature does seem to have the effect of the participant finding his or her limits. From this perspective the experience is valid as very few people would even contemplate embarking on such a course of action let alone attain partial if not complete success. Rob wrote the following account subsequent to my return and after the first meeting we had at home where we tried to bring the whole experience out into the open and deal with our feelings on the subject. I have to say this initial encounter was not that successful but it was a start. Rob Ringer: -

You will all have read the tiring and exhausting account of Richard's solo attempt, and some of you will be aware of the continuing problems encountered with the Challenge Business. I apologise to many of you who did not receive my account from El Hierro regarding my retirement from the race.

Coming back to Cumbria was hard enough in itself for me, and to be honest I had no desire to return. Even harder was the weekend just spent with Rich and Usha, with me knowing we had to discuss the situation, but not making the first moves to clarify and explain my perception.

Hindsight is a wonderful luxury, things should have been different, and the fact is that they are not. This was a team effort, and I continue to recognise the enormous effort Richard put into the whole project, and I had always considered him to be the lead partner in the venture, due to his previous experience at sea, and outstanding organisational abilities. This makes it all the harder to come to terms with the fact that a project jointly nurtured and developed over three years, came to a premature end. A fact that I must take responsibility for, and will live with me for a very long time, knowing that personal and public support had been willing us to succeed. Not for one minute did I think that after such a short time I would become psychologically frozen so to speak. The race start was confusing enough with the start line changing almost daily, and the whole area of communication systems never being adequately resolved. Despite being the first boat to be scrutinised and have it's Inmarset system wired, as late as Saturday, October 6th, we were still having problems with the messaging service, and occasionally the Palm top would give a totally erroneous position. Only after Matthew Ratsey plugged the system into his own 'lap-top' and the Inmarset showed our true position did we feel a little more confident. We also spent the week prior to leaving working out a coded system of messages for ourselves, apart from the one supplied by the CB, to message home base. It was also the time we found out that we could only text a message with 56 characters and not the original 200 we had been led to believe. At such a late hour in the proceedings, the tendency was to say that we would just cope with it. Departure day was highly charged emotionally for both of us, but I believe we left in high spirits and decided early on as to what our rowing regime would be. My own brief note in my diary mention starting in fair conditions, but by the evening they had deteriorated considerably. Other accounts have mentioned our meeting with the Gomera ferry. The next three days all I can recall doing is rowing and sleeping, putting out the sea anchor and pulling it back in. We had seen the Challenge yacht I believe on the Monday, the second day, not on the third day as is reported by the CB. However I would defer to them if they have this on record. That apart, Rich called on the VHF to inform them that the palm top was not working and we were unable to send or receive messages, their clear reply was that they would return in a few hours. They did not and we next saw them on Saturday at El Hierro after they had been contacted on our behalf. As I have said very little apart from rowing and sleeping happened on those three days for me, eating was almost out of the question as the desire to consume anything was not there. We did nibble on small items, and the one morning we did force ourselves to eat, the taste of the food for me only made me vomit. I was managing the other effects of seasickness by wearing a slow release patch behind my ear. I was not dogged by the same totally overpowering sickness that beset our first sea trial at Plymouth.

Feeling totally exhausted and spent, I sat at the oars on the Wednesday, only to put them down as Rich emerged from the cabin to say that I needed a rest because of exhaustion. His comment to me was that he was 'not sure that we would do this', my immediate reply agreed with that. With hindsight I believe Rich said this due to my almost total lack of communication during those first three days, and my general demeanour. The lack of communication was not intended, I merely tried to keep things together so that I could row. Once I had said this I went into shut down mode. I still find it extremely difficult to describe the range of emotions that I experienced as we sat at anchor for nearly two days, messaging a yacht with no success. Could I have changed my mind? Yes I could, but I could not step outside of the situation and look at it rationally. The failure to do so is acutely painful, and has subsequently made me query my own esteem. This does not justify my actions, but out there that was all I could do. I simply could not row in an westerly direction. On the Friday as were unable to raise anyone or anything either on the palm top or VHF, and as we were not in the position of a 'marine emergency' we took the decision to row back to El Hierro to take stock. Rich notes that my demeanour improved on the return row, as I was determined to get us back safely. Once on dry land could I have changed my mind and got back on the boat? Yes, I suppose I could, but I had made a decision and I stuck to it, as in some ways I did not want to trust myself not to falter again. My concern then was to ensure that once Rich had decided to go solo that everything I could do on the boat to assist in a solo row was in order for such an endeavour. I hope that in some way this explains my retirement from the race, and know that I bear an overpowering sense of failure for letting my friend and rowing partner down during the opportunity of a lifetime.

Since the first time Rob and I met after my return, we have been in touch and had a couple more opportunities to discuss things together. My gut feeling is that an experience of this nature, whilst extremely profound and deep, should not end up ruining many great years of friendship, not only between us but our respective families as well. The nature of the relationship had changed anyway, with our children growing up, but as time passes and a little work is done I see no reason why the patient should not be declared fit and healthy again even if the surgery leaves a few scars to remind us of what went before.

It wasn't all bad despite what has already been said. The sea can be a captivating place and the wildlife breathtaking. I remember on one occasion during the weather at the start, surfing down a wave and seeing several dolphins jumping out of the face and 'flying' parallel to the boat before disappearing back into their watery home. Ironically the night we rowed back to El Hierro was magnificent! It was totally calm until dawn and the sky was perfectly clear exposing a myriad of stars as the galaxies stretched away into infinity. With no light pollution or sound the experience was magical when you stopped rowing and looked and listened. Even when we were rowing, bright phosphorescence lit the water like a thousand jewels with each stroke. It is times like these that make you want to return to the ocean. Ironic that the best night's row was as we were in retreat!

Finally in this chapter is the text of an email I received from a fellow competitor on my return, who had heard about our experiences and had had similar problems with the text messaging service. I have included this partly to show we were not the only ones left in this position but also because in the event of it having worked the outcome may have been very different. I will give my reason for this at the conclusion of the narrative and I will make this the last major reference to the text messaging at the risk of boring you to much with it. However it was a major factor in the failure of the enterprise and informs the debate about communications and ocean rowing.

Richard

Commiserations regarding your withdrawal. Fantastic effort however in being gutsy enough to get there in the first place, and facing the challenge single handed after your problems.

I am writing because I have just recently had the opportunity to browse the WEARC site and read the press releases etc. Like you, we started the race using the Inmarsat D communicator as our sole means of long range communications, under the assumption that the system was fault free as implied by the information provided to us by World Cruising via the Challenge Business. Unfortunately, also had a lot of problems with the Inmarsat D unit. I thought you might be interested in hearing about our experiences with the Inmarsat D+ and our dealings with World Cruising.

*Prior to the race start we quickly realised that there were a number of problems with the Inmarsat D units. As this was our only long range communications equipment, we went to great lengths to sort out the problems with James Hall and Challenge Business. Unfortunately, we discovered that insufficient testing of the units had been undertaken prior to the race, and that nobody at World Cruising or Challenge Business really understood the Inmarsat D clearly. At race start on Oct 7, we were aware that the units would not send, but we were under the understanding that we could receive messages. James Hall was also aware that the units would not send, as we spoke over the phone only the day before. (I find it interesting that James failed to inform you prior to the race that he knew the units were unable to send). We were happy with this arrangement, as we primarily wanted the communicator to receive weather and race position data. Unfortunately, when at sea we discovered that the communicators were unable not only to send but also unable to receive messages. Our registered user, who was tasked with sending us weather information, identified within the first week that we were not receiving the messages. Over the next week and a half, our registered user was (to put it lightly) ****** around by World Cruising, who refused to believe that the system was not operating correctly, and refused to accept responsibility for the problems. It was not until we were visited by the Challenge Business yacht, almost 3 weeks into the race, that we were able to confirm that we were not receiving messages. Interestingly enough, when we were visited, the Challenge Business safety yacht informed us that no crews who were using the communicator had successfully received messages, and that they had known for some time that a software problem was to blame. World Cruising would have known about this software problem since the start of the race. Despite this knowledge, World Cruising never informed us at the race start and during the first 3 weeks of the race, stating that the reason we were not receiving messages was that our registered user was sending the messages incorrectly. This caused great concern to our registered user, who worked exceptionally hard but unsuccessfully to correct a problem, which unbeknown to him, World Cruising knew all the time could not be corrected.*

As you've probably noticed, I'm fairly disappointed in the behaviour displayed by World Cruising and the Challenge Business regarding the Inmarsat Communicator. Besides the lack of weather information representing a performance disadvantage during the race, I'm also disappointed in the lack of preparation/ testing of the unit prior to the race and the poor service and technical support offered with the units. But most of all I'm disappointed in the lack of responsibility and blame shifting, which caused unnecessary distress to our registered user.

Chapter Thirteen

My mind was made up to attempt the row solo by the time we reached La Restinga on El Hierro. As we rowed in to the little port we seemed to be back to square one again, but as often seems to be the case at a time of need, individuals turn up who are able to help and encourage you to press on. Loads happened and people came out of the woodwork even before we had moored alongside the fishing quay. The rest of the story is probably best told by the diary entry I made on my return home, so I will turn to this to recount the events of the final week.

Rower's Diary Thursday, October 25th, 2001

Here I am safe and sound back at home in Worcester. I flew in to Heathrow from Tenerife via Madrid on Wednesday night having caught the Sea Cat ferry from La Gomera at 1000 hours that morning. Its fantastic to be home again and I have been overwhelmed by the kindness and good wishes that so many people have sent.

I thought I should recount the final part of the story whilst it is still fresh in my mind.

My last diary entry was from Babette's computer on El Hierro, the most westerly Canary Island marked on ancient charts as 'The End of the World', in the light of experience this is quite an appropriate title! (You may remember Babette was 'The English Lady' who helped us out from her home in La Restinga, she was brilliant! She also has a room for hire if anyone fancies visiting this fascinating island unspoilt by the tourist industry)

After our arrival back at Estaca on El Hierro we were met by Challenge Business 47 one of the yachts following the race. They towed us on the Sunday up to La Restinga at the other end of the Island whilst trying to effect repairs on our texting equipment. By the time we got there the system was still not working and the yacht had to go off and tend to some other ailing competitors. We had slept on the yacht overnight and before leaving to enter La Restinga on The Spirit, I was asked to sign a 'disclaimer' about the increased dangers of attempting a single handed row. As I had had a long discussion with the Project Manager Teresa Evans about this and subsequently emailed her stating my expectations for the attempt I was happy to do this in the knowledge support would still be available and if it had to be withdrawn I would be informed beforehand so I could decide whether or not to continue under such circumstances.

My solo row now depended on two things, firstly getting hold of some substantial and effective alternative means of communication in the form of a satellite phone and secondly that it would be delivered in time for me to still have a chance of leaving whilst I still had the assurance that CB safety cover was within reach. I set a departure deadline for the following Wednesday. My wife

Usha, along with some of the fantastic people who have assisted us, managed to procure the said phone on the Monday and arranged for one of the guys from the team who had worked on our solar rig to bring it out to El Hierro. Sven arrived on Wednesday morning and by the evening everything was installed and working. It was time to go. I had a beer with Sven and Rob, rang Ush from the boat to do a final check to ensure the phone was working and at 2100 hours switched on my navigation lights and equipment and pulled back out into the Atlantic alone.

At this point Rob has sent his thoughts on this moment of departure, so here is his contribution:

On Wednesday 17th at approximately 9.15pm Rich firmly attached his safety line to his life jacket as a warm south westerly wind blew into the harbour of La Restinga. Not the best direction to be rowing into, but neither was it hard enough to prevent the departure of the Spirit of Worcestershire, with its captain, on it's attempt on the Atlantic Ocean. The hours prior to this had been tense, with the fitting of the newly acquired satellite phone, the final checking of messages on e-mail and last minute phone calls home. There was boat talk as we walked around from the bar where Rich had enjoyed a cold beer, his last for an unspecified number of days. Sven, who had delivered the phone accompanied us, Geoff, a Belgium yacht owner, voluntarily exiled in La Restinga, and a local hippy. I accompanied Rich onto the Spirit of Worcestershire, stowed some final items and locked the oars into place whilst he made a final check on the GPS. He emerged from the cabin and clipped on. We then hugged like long lost brothers, for my part not really wanting to let go. Words cannot adequately describe the depth of feeling expressed by friends in that moment. Whether Barbados is attained may be unimportant in some respects, because out there is a man of passion and commitment who not only wishes to achieve for himself and his family, but also for his community, and I perhaps have more reason to be humbled by that and count it a privilege to be his friend. As Richard has already urged the community in his last piece to dig deep for St Richards, I would endorse that, and repeat my final words as he rowed out of the harbour, 'Godspeed Rich'.

My diary continues: -

The rapturous applause of the three people who saw me off were soon lost to the sounds of the sea and the light SW wind (blowing the wrong way and apparently most unusual for those parts.) With darkness all around and the safe haven of the little harbour slowly becoming just a collection of lights over a restless sea a hundred thoughts began to press in on me, what sort of rowing regime should I impose upon myself, how far would I get each day, what should I aim for so I didn't spend the rest of my life out there? I had a good row overnight and made substantial progress. The island was getting smaller and it's features becoming less defined a sure sign of progress. Then the wind increased from the South, exactly the opposite direction from where it needed to be. I began to loose the ground I had made the night before. The wind increased and I began to be pushed back towards the island. Looking at the track on the GPS navigator I was surprised to see that I was also being pushed in a westerly direction at right angles to the wind! This meant I was gradually being pushed towards the island and along it's coastline to it's most remote headland. This continued overnight and before sunrise I was getting worried that on my present track I would end up wrecked on the rocky, isolated volcanic shore of El Hierro. I collected a variety of flares from my pack and waited to see what would happen next as there seemed to be a strange current that refused to let me get further from the danger of the island's coast no matter how hard I rowed. The sun rose and I was relieved to see I was actually further off the coast than I previously thought, I put the flares away....for the time being.

Alone on the Atlantic.

The SW wind meant losing a great deal of ground and I spent all day trying to fight this situation. I then decided to alter course and head due South, the wind abated and I started to make progress once again and eventually got back onto my original course of 223 degrees. I reckon I did about 20 miles but only gained 10 in distance! I was very tired, an all-pervading tiredness, not the kind you feel after a hard day at work! I decided to sleep but with the wind increasing again I deployed the parachute anchor. Spent a very windy night on the anchor.

I got up at 0200 on Friday morning and had some breakfast, the wind was blowing at about 7 knots from the SW ie right against me for the direction I wanted to go. You can't really row one of these boats against a wind like this as you will make little progress and kill yourself physically, so rowing was out of the question. A squall then blew up so I left the parachute out.

Usha and I had decided I'd ring home at 0800 each morning so I did and said I'd carry on despite all the difficulties. I had brought the parachute in, an exhausting task in the wind but soon had to deploy it again, it was incredibly frustrating and tiring. At 1330 the wind suddenly changed to the NE, exactly the right direction for me to gain ground! I retrieved the chute and shot off in the right direction. The wind was up to about force 4 and the boat flew along. For a time I was really enjoying the ride! At 1600 hours the wind went to the North and rowing became more difficult with a confused sea. I had some food I really didn't want.

By Saturday morning the boat was drifting in a force 4, it should have been going in the direction I wanted but once again the current had better ideas and I lost 5 miles of the ground I had just covered. Anyway I had been told one of the Challenge Business support vessels would visit me to check on my progress. As I hadn't seen anything but sea for the last three days I thought this would be a pleasant diversion. I made steady progress when rowing but my morale was getting low as I realised that every time I stopped for a rest I was losing all I had gained and as a single hander there is no one else to keep up the momentum and eventually get out of the currents that were besetting me. Teresa Evans rang to say the yacht would not be with me until the next day and I rang a guy called John Searson who did the race single handed in 1997 when his partner had to be taken off through injury. He said he thought I was caught in local currents even though I was now some 30 miles off El Hierro but if I just let the boat drift with the wind when I was resting, I should gain ground! The reality was somewhat different. I didn't deploy the parachute again to see what would happen and sure enough I began to creep North again back towards the island even though I had a stiff breeze that should have been blowing me South. I gave up and deployed the para to see if that would help but it didn't.

On Sunday not only had we continued back North and lost more ground but the boat had suddenly done an elongated figure of 8 around my course line! The current then took me west about 4-5 miles from the course. I tried to 'go with the flow' and made some progress albeit in a different direction than I had planned. I had spoken to Ush the night before about the possibility of giving up but I rang Teresa Evans about lunch time to say I was feeling a bit more encouraged and if the yacht visit was delayed that would be OK. She then told me the yacht was 300 miles away and would not be visiting me, rather strange as the last time we spoke the yacht was allegedly in La Gomera re fuelling before heading back out to the main fleet and visiting me on the way. I was devastated by this news which flew in the face of the email I had specifically sent to request a visit early on in the single handed row to check how I was doing. I thought the Challenge Business had agreed to this but I guess this is the Challenge Business….need I say more! After this news, the fact that having thought I had made good progress, I had only covered about 5 miles and was again losing that because of the current, I started to experience a sense of real despair. I then boiled some water to make soup and put the mug on the hatch to pick up the soup packet, the boat lurched and the boiling water fell onto the back of my left hand. It was agony compounded by the fact that I then had to extract the medical kit from the bow locker, drag it across the deck to the aft cabin, take out all 5 containers from the sea bag, find the right dressings and cream and do something about my condition whilst my skin fell off and the pain increased! That was the final straw, I rang Usha and said I had decide to throw in the towel. She said she would support my decision. I then called Teresa and she said she would make local arrangements from El Hierro for the following day to have me towed back.

I rang Teresa at 0900 as arranged for an update, she informed me they were still trying to contact the right people and would get back to me as soon as she had news but assured me I would be back in El Hierro by the end of the day. Having heard nothing by 1200 hours I rang the CB again but Teresa said she still hadn't been able to complete arrangements and would call me once this was done. Later in the afternoon she rang back and said nobody was willing to come out that far and tow me back but she had arranged for a helicopter to come and winch me off! This was devastating news as I was under the impression that the CB would assist and until the day before I believed a yacht was in the vicinity! Now it looked like I was going to have to abandon the boat and be lifted off with nothing but a handful of dubious memories. The depth of despair at this prospect was very deep as I still had £15,000 to pay off on the whole project and this was all tied up in the boat. This course of action would have serious consequences for the future; it all seemed a bit drastic. The boats were not insured whilst at sea and the CB would not allow them to be left unattended saying this would contravene maritime law as they would present a hazard to navigation so burning was the only option! I asked Teresa to contact the rescue people to see if they would allow anything to be taken off the boat with me and to give me an hour or so to contemplate my fate, I didn't refuse the assistance at this point, I just felt that perhaps there was another option. I then spoke to the real star of this whole episode Usha, who was not only extremely annoyed about this outcome but also intent on seeing if she could come up with an alternative. Particularly as most of effective work up to and during the project has been in spite of rather than due to the race 'organisers'. She rang Kenneth Crutchlow of the Ocean Rowing Society and he immediately got onto the case. Within an hour and after various frantic phone calls to the Challenge Business to try and ascertain the insurance situation, Doug and Anita Carroll and a guy called Neil left La Gomera on a power boat in deteriorating conditions agreed to come to my aid. Usha rang me with the good news followed by a call from Teresa who said they should be with me the following morning. Usha then rang to say they had just left and would be with me in about 4 hours. I settled down to wait but the wind was picking up so I left the parachute out. At 1930 hours I brought the para in and at 2015 set off a white flare to help detect my position. I immediately regretted retrieving the para as the wind was increasing to force 5-6 with breaking waves. I was not sure what to do, if I re deployed the anchor Doug might arrive and I'd have the even more exhausting task of heaving it in against ever increasing wind conditions, on the other hand if he had been delayed it would be unwise not to err on the side of caution. I decided to re deploy and having crawled up the deck with my left hand giving me considerable pain, the phone rang!!

It was Usha who informed me Doug had been delayed by the deteriorating conditions and would not be there until around midnight. I gave her my up to date position as I had drifted some 5 miles NW of the previous one and made the point that I was still going NW. I crawled out again and deployed the chute, immediately bringing the bow into the weather and making a more comfortable and more importantly safe ride.

I settled down to wait with the VHF radio on channel 16 the internationally recognised channel for keeping a radio watch and emergency frequency. With the wind howling outside and regular wave whooshing down and smacking against the cabin side I was glad to have the chute out and felt relatively secure and calm. At 2330 hours there was a faint bit of static on the VHF that could only mean someone was within about 3 miles of my position. I leapt out of the cabin and tried to call them. Within a few minutes they were within range and I made the point that the parachute was out and not to come too close until I had retrieved it. They asked me to do this and then set off a white flare to pin point my position. The retrieval in those conditions was an absolutely exhausting process but I eventually made it and ignited the flare. We made definite contact and within a few minutes the lights bobbing away at some distance turned into the substantial bulk of the cruiser Jantonee. They came alongside which was quite intimidating when you consider the boat was about three times the height of the Spirit if not more. We secured alongside with both boats being thrown around all over the place and crashing against the fenders on Jantonee's side or missing and hitting the hull. It took up to half an hour to prepare the tow and then I had to jump aboard before the tow could commence. I met the crew and expressed my heartfelt thanks for the huge commitment and

'The Spirit' in tow back to the Canaries.

The author's bandaged and painful hand!

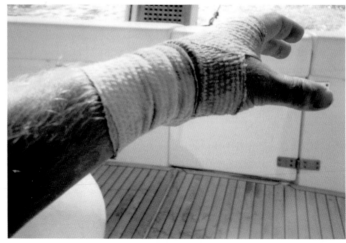

courage they had demonstrated in coming to my aid in such poor conditions. I then went below had a can of beer and fell sound asleep I was utterly exhausted!

The 35 mile tow back to La Restinga continued whilst I slept and we entered the port at first light to re fuel. As soon as this was complete and we had bought a few things to eat we set off for La Gomera. The wind had come up to a gale as soon as we left the port and we proceeded at around 3-4 knots with the tow holding very well, although the Spirit kept disappearing from view behind the waves as we progressed. Fortunately once off the coast of El Hierro the wind decreased somewhat and conditions improved. We were eventually able to increase speed to around 8 knots and completed the 50 mile journey, arriving in San Sebastian at about 1900 hours. Doug, Anita and Neil had faced very poor conditions and a round trip of 180 miles to come to my assistance. They were hugely encouraging at all times and very positive about what I had achieved. They considered I had made the right decision and were more than happy to come to my assistance. I will be ever grateful to them for this and can only offer very warm and heartfelt thanks for their enormous efforts not only through bringing me back safely but the boat as well. I also have to say a HUGE THANK YOU to

Doug steers 'Jantonee' into the safety of San Sebastian.

Doug & Anita: the author's heroes!

Kenneth for supporting Usha by intervening on our behalf in a difficult situation and of course to Usha who is the most fantastic wife in the world.

So the great Atlantic adventure finally came to an end as I boarded the Sea Cat Ferry to Tenerife and the flights home. The Spirit of Worcestershire remains in the care of Doug and Anita on the hard in La Gomera waiting for shipment back to the UK. I am home, tired, grateful to be alive and will now attempt to make sense of it all. I'm no hero, just an ordinary sort of guy hoping to get a little extra out of life for me and for others. Do I have any regrets, probably, although it is too early to say what they may be. I am unsure about the way ahead; I feel the lessons that can be learned from my experience should not be lost by the euphoria that may surround the successful attempts of other teams to complete the crossing. I am concerned that any attempt to do this will be brushed aside by certain parties as sour grapes or a lack of some kind of misguided machismo.

To end on a more positive note, the thing I have really enjoyed about this Challenge has been the people. I have met so many good-hearted folks along the way, ever since starting the whole project in June 1998. In a world where things seem to be going completely mad and individuals full of bitterness, resentment, hatred and fear think they have some kind of right to wreck the lives of others they never even met, I have been privileged to meet and work with so many who display the exact opposite of this kind of attitude. Kind, generous, enthusiastic, courageous individuals who really desire to support this crazy guy no matter what the outcome. I particularly want to thank my wife Usha and my children Nayna, John and Joshua, everyone who makes up the wonderful institution of St Richard's Hospice and the work they do, my employers, The Worcestershire Youth Service, friends and relations. During the actual race period I have to say thanks to Kenneth and the good services of the ORS, Babette on El Hierro, Doug, Anita and Neil for rescuing me. Thanks also to the Ward Evans race sponsors and Appeal PR for salvaging things at the start and treating us rowers with some respect. I must of course give a special mention to my rowing partner Rob. He gave it his best shot. Sometimes things in life don't work out quite how we planned, perhaps its the journey that is more important than the destination and what we learn along the way. Rob has been a good friend for over 20 years, good friends are hard to find and whilst I am disappointed that we didn't make it, I hold no malice towards him. I trust we are big enough to overcome the feelings of sadness, discouragement and perhaps failure, in the realisation that in the final analysis it is important to hang on to the deeper things in life, like friendship and reconciliation.

In the end, who was the final winner? I guess the answer is the Atlantic Ocean. You can never conquer or win unless the Ocean lets you. Even those rowing heroes who continue to battle their way across, will only get there if the Atlantic is kind and allows them to succeed. When you are out there alone and you see the awesome power of the elements around you it is a very humbling experience. I am very grateful that the Atlantic was kind to me and let me come home. Its mighty power is indeed awesome!

Doug gives the author a tow after refuelling at La Restinga en route back to La Gomera after the 2001 asttempt was abandoned.

The author rows out into the Atlantic at the start of the Ocean Rowing Society Atlantic Rowing Regatta.

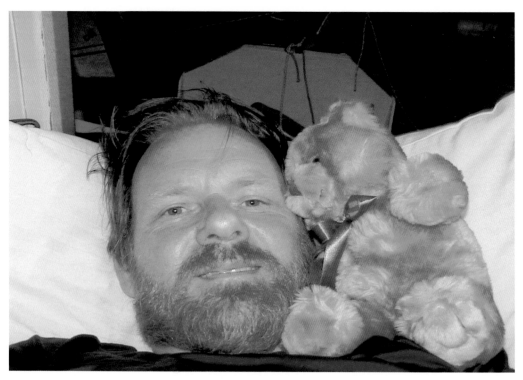

The author's faithful companion & mascot, 'Dougan', a greatly valued gift from Doug & Anita.

The author visited by 'Kilcullen', seven weeks after starting his epic row.

Taking a wave, seven weeks out.

The occasional welcome visitor!

The author takes the tow from 'Kilcullen' after 100 days at sea.

A last look back as Phil helps the author aboard 'Kilcullen'.

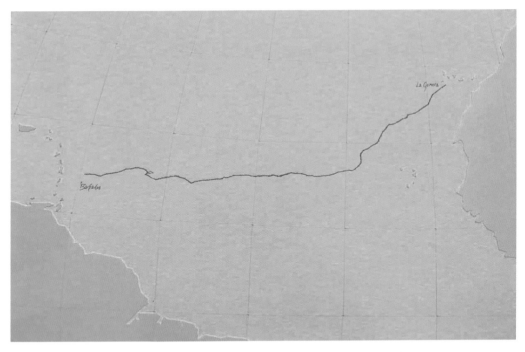

The author's long, hard, route across the Atlantic.

A warm welcome for the author aboard 'Kilcullen'.

Victory after 101 days at sea!

Richard, Dougan & 'Najojo': The Magnificent Three?

The author reunited with Usha, and Josh with a flying fish, at Port St Charles.

The author contemplates 3,430 nautical miles of achievement.

11th person in history to successfully row this Atlantic route solo.

The author back home in Worcester.

Atlantic sunset, 1000 miles from land.

Big Atlantic rollers obscure the sunset.

Sunset as a weather front moves overhead.

Ever changing scenes of natural beauty.

Another spectacular performance on nature's immense stage.

Another multi-media presentation in the author's hectic programme.

*The author receives a trophy and certificate from his good friend Kenneth
Crutchlow at the Ocean Rowing Society Dinner in London.*

*I did it!
A fitting end to a great
adventure.*

Chapter Fourteen

That could have been the end of the story but I came home with an acute awareness that I still had unfinished business. I can't say I immediately decided to get back into the nearest boat and try again, far from it, but there was something inside that felt deeply unsatisfied with the outcome of this first attempt. I had a sense of incompleteness, a feeling that although the experience had been really tough, especially due to the nature of all that had happened, somehow I still felt the goal was still achievable despite everything.

It was strange coming home, everyone was so supportive, and it almost felt like I had actually got across! The local media in particular were taken with my story and everything that appeared in the press and on radio had a positive edge to it. Lots of people wanted to know more about what exactly had happened and offered bucket loads of sympathy whilst being full of admiration that I had even tried in the first place. This goodwill extended to Rob as well, though many who talked to me were obviously fascinated by the dynamics of our relationship now the attempt was all over. This was a difficult one for me, as I honestly didn't know at that point how I felt about Rob. Part of me wanted everything to be as it had always been, with Rob remaining one of my best friends, but for true relationships to survive they need nurture and Rob hadn't been in touch since his return to see how I was getting on. This did become a bit of a problem. I tried to put a brave face on it and clung to fairly bland responses to questions like 'How do you feel about Rob? Have you been in touch since you came back?' But deep down I knew that sooner or later this had to be tackled full on. I guess I was hoping that Rob would make the first move as I considered this would have been the 'honourable' thing to do under the circumstances. In the end we heard nothing and I knew I would have to move first, in fact it was Usha who pushed me to face up to inviting Rob and Therese down for a weekend so that we could at least try and begin to address all that had happened and come to terms with how it had affected us both.

In the end I called Rob and asked him and Therese to come down to Worcester for a weekend. They accepted but when they arrived it was a very strained affair and only at the last minute, on the Sunday afternoon, did any full and frank discussion begin. It unearthed many of the things that had been a problem even before we had left for the Canaries. I can't say that prior to our departure I had felt any major hassles with Rob but in retrospect there were probably things that should have been talked about and resolved at the time.

Rob's major input had been to the boat building project and his contacts had led to the support of the Sport's Scientists, he had made a major commitment to the training programme and did get involved with the occasional Hospice meeting or project fund raiser. However I had always driven the project a bit like a dog with a bone! This became a bit of a double edged sword, especially for my nearest and dearest, and I think the constant pressure of preparing the project alongside the Hospice fund raising and profiling events took their toll on my relationship with my immediate family. I don't think my relationship with Usha was on the rocks but perhaps there was the threat of danger a little way off and I was unwilling or too busy to identify it as such. The fact is that I cannot speak too highly of my wife's fortitude, commitment, support and love throughout the whole of this very long project. She is a very special person and without her I probably wouldn't have reached my final goal. Recently someone said "I reckon you two could achieve anything you set your mind to", well I'm not sure about that but I understand the sentiment as together Usha and I are a pretty formidable force! Usha is a bit like the fuel in a vehicle, you never see it but without it you'll get nowhere fast! I think she felt that I had carried more than my fair share of the project and if Rob had given a little more input, especially after we had launched the boat, it would have relieved the pressure on me and consequently on her as well.

Rob couldn't explain why he had felt and acted as he had done once at sea and whilst he didn't think it could have been any different, the reasons for his behaviour eluded him. I could see his anguish as he struggled to make sense of it all but I don't think he could, and as he left that Sunday afternoon to head back to Cumbria the outcome of this initial meeting felt unsatisfactory with an all pervading sense of sadness. Had this potential adventure of a lifetime only ended in tears and the destruction of a relationship I had valued so highly? I hoped this was not the case and that time would indeed be the great healer. Since then I have seen Rob on a couple of occasions and each time I have felt things were improving, maybe the next row would help us both to 'find' each other again? Only time would tell.

After a few weeks at home I started to yearn for a way to continue on the hard road to success on the other side of the mighty Atlantic Ocean. I had the opportunity to go to the Paris Boat Show with Kenneth Crutchlow and visit a stand with a French prototype rowing boat designed for a proposed race for solo rowers across the North Atlantic. I had a vague idea that I might enter this and that the trip to Paris would help me make up my mind whether or not this was a viable proposition. I am not sure my first visit to Paris could have been described as romantic, but Kenneth's company was as convivial as ever and our discussions ranged wide over issues relating to future aspirations for the Ocean Rowing Society and the possibility of our own race across the ocean in 2004. I came home having decided the French option was not for me, which was just as well as the actual event never materialised.

I had talked to Kenneth about commissioning a new boat to a new design that he hoped would become the basic vessel for future ORS events. I knew this was going to represent a major financial commitment probably around £60,000 and at this point I was £10,000 in debt with 'The Spirit of Worcestershire' and all her equipment still out in La Gomera. The prospect of achieving this seemed somewhat unrealistic but I have always enjoyed rising to a challenge! I needed to get 'The Spirit' back to the UK and sell her in order to pay off this debt and draw a line under the old project. Then I could concentrate on trying to put the new build project together. In the end it took six months to get the boat back and it wasn't until the end of 2003 that I was able to sell the boat and balance the books.

I had tried to start raising finance for the new build project and even been down to Exmouth a couple of times to the boat builder's yard to see the new design fibre glass hull taking shape. This boat was the first of the 'new breed' of ocean rowing boats and a Russian who intended to do a solo row over the Canary to Barbados route had commissioned her. The hull design looked great and I really wanted to become the proud owner of the next vessel to attempt the same challenge. However the time and tide wait for no man and it was becoming more apparent by the day that raising funds for the row was going to be nigh on impossible, especially as many of my contacts locally had already donated funds for the last attempt and were unlikely to do so again.

Whilst all this was going on, a few of us connected with the ORS had been hatching a plan with Kenneth to organise our own race open to solo and double rowing crews, with the possibility of the new design hull being fitted out for a four man attempt as well. I had offered Kenneth my help with the organisation of the race and was happy to share the expertise I had gained from the previous 4 years experience. I had also talked to him about the prospect of my own entry becoming more doubtful with no finance forthcoming and time running out. I had not registered as yet for the race, which was now a viable proposition with preparations well underway as it would have been a bit hard to attempt it without a boat! Kenneth then offered me the use of an existing boat under a rental agreement that belonged to the ORS. He was unsure of what sort of state this boat would be in as she had already done the Trade Winds route twice and was now being used as a training boat in the Isle of Man. Suddenly the possibility of being able to enter the race as a solo rower came within my grasp, providing that this boat was still sea worthy. The only way to ascertain this was to take a trip out to the Isle of Man to give the boat a thorough inspection.

Matt Murfitt had entered the next Challenge Business race scheduled for 2003, and was in the process of building a new boat from a standard kit similar to the one Rob and I had used for the 2001 race. He was based in a little seaside town on the Isle of Man called Peel. I flew out from Birmingham on Thursday, April 1st, 2003, and was met at the airport by Matt's wife who took me back to their place. Matt was at work and so I followed her directions to the boat which was moored at the landward end of the little harbour. To seaward lay the imposing remains of the ancient Castle and ruined Cathedral on St. Patrick's Isle. Here the first Irish missionaries arrived in the middle of the fifth century. This little isle was to become a base for Viking settlers and a fort of timber, or pile, was built thus giving Peel its name.

It was a bleak day, punctuated by wind driven sheets of icy rain from leaden skies. The place was almost deserted as I made my way to find 'Odessa', formerly 'Hospicare', abandoned on the harbour mud by the ebbing tide. I climbed down a slippery ladder and stepped onto the small motorboat moored against the harbour wall, I gingerly crossed the deck and lowered myself over the side and onto the rowing boat in eager anticipation of whether this rather sad looking craft had the potential to fulfil my dream.

At first glance she looked somewhat forlorn. Chunks of wood were missing from the gunwales and the well in front of the cabin hatch had water sloshing about in it. The paintwork left much to be desired and there was sand everywhere. Inside the hatches lay rubble sacks full of gravel that were being used to ballast the boat and the makeshift rowing positions had great lumps of wood screwed over them as a temporary solution for a two man crew to propel her through the water.

The boat that could make the whole dream come true, lying in the little harbour of Peel.

Inside the cabin lay an old car battery used to power an even older GPS unit and cabin lighting, to enable the guys to see what they were doing when out on the briny deep after dark. The electrical system looked completely shot and would need stripping out and replacing. I spent a couple of hours both inside the cabin and out on deck dodging the showers, as I inspected every inch of the boat. I opened every hatch and mopped out the water checking for leaks. It was imperative to ascertain whether or not the hull structure was sound. Eventually I reached the conclusion that despite her rather sorry state of neglect she was basically well built and seaworthy. With a major refit and make over I saw no reason why I couldn't build a lasting relationship with her that would sustain us both across the wild wastes of the Atlantic Ocean. With a growing sense of excited anticipation I made my way back to Matt's house to meet the man himself.

I spent a convivial evening with him and his potential rowing partner at a quayside pub and we discussed every aspect of the project he was putting together and the arrangements he had made with Kenneth regarding return of the boat. It transpired that the agreed period of the boat loan was almost up and responsibility for getting her back to the mainland lay with Matt. He said he would bring the boat to Worcester as soon as possible and would try and arrange free passage on one of the Manx ferries. He was concerned that the TT Races would tie up any available space in the not to distant future so he was keen to get on with the sorting out a deal as quickly as possible.

I stayed overnight with the Murfitts and flew out the following day bound for Birmingham Airport in the knowledge that I had a boat for the challenge and I could now officially register my entry. Unfortunately nothing is ever simple and I became increasingly concerned over the next few weeks about the fact that the boat was still in the middle of the Irish Sea!

In the meantime Kenneth had been in touch to ask if I would be prepared to fly out to the Channel Islands and inspect another boat on behalf of a chap called Louis Ginglo, who was travelling the world with his wife Ellie. Louis had been negotiating the purchase of one of two boats built in Jersey for previous Challenge events. She belonged to Kerry Bladin and Louis wanted an independent assessment of her ability to do the job.

On Wednesday, April 23rd, I found myself back at Birmingham Airport waiting for a plane to Jersey. Kerry met me at the airport after an uneventful flight and took me straight up to the boat, which was kept outside a rather precarious looking farm shed. I had a good look over her, especially the rather novel foot operated steering gear. She was well built and in good condition although everything had been sheathed in fibreglass, which made for a very strong boat but also a heavy one. However, if the main aim was to stay alive this was probably as good a boat as any to set off in.

I took copious photographs so that I could email them with a report to Louis, and then spent a very pleasant evening with Kerry and his wife at a local restaurant. I stayed over in a hotel and flew out again the next day having successfully completed my task. Well almost, once Louis had made his final decision there was the small matter of getting her across to the mainland. This was starting to become a habit!

After all this island hopping and boat inspecting it felt like time for a little light relief! On Friday, May 16th, 2003, this came in the form of the inaugural Ocean Rowing Society black tie dinner at the Army & Navy Club on Pall Mall in London. It was a very splendid venue; even the paintings depicting death and destruction from our 'glorious' past added a certain *je ne sais quoi* from an artistic perspective! I had hired the relevant bib and tucker from a place in Worcester, as this kind of regalia isn't something I would normally wear even though I look the part when I do! It was a very pleasant and successful evening with an excellent dinner washed down with copious amounts of red and white wine, culminating in the awarding of certificates recognising the achievements of the assembled rowing crews. Even I got one, although my attempt had got me only a comparatively short distance from the start line. I probably should have felt a bit of a fraud but it had been a long hard road to the start line in 2001, and possibly even harder once we set out with all that ensued, so it was nice to have had my efforts acknowledged in some way, even if the certificate didn't record a completed row with the time it had taken as those with a more successful outcome received.

Back in Worcester I was becoming increasingly anxious about the lack of a boat appearing from the Isle of Man. I had spoken to Matt on a number of occasions and each time he insisted that he was making some progress with transportation but was still having difficulty in getting a free passage to the mainland. This combined with the build up to the TT Races now in full swing meant that this scenario was becoming more and more unlikely. Then out of the blue I received a phone call from Matt's wife telling me he had sustained and survived a heart attack whilst in the kitchen at home! My first reaction to this was one of great sorrow, I knew how much work is involved in putting together an ocean rowing project and with all the stresses involved the last thing you want is a breakdown of your health, even more so if the result forces you to abandon something that takes your whole life over. In the case of the Challenge Races dealing with something like this was made worse by the high financial implications if you had to withdraw from the event, which was a decision Matt was now faced with. Outside of my concern for Matt's health and well being I was still conscious of the fact that I did not have a boat and once I did there would be a considerable amount of work that needed doing to bring her up to spec for the 2004 Regatta. I didn't want to add to Matt's distress by putting more pressure on him, so I decided to bite the bullet and hope that he would soon be fit enough to make some alternative arrangements to deliver the boat to Worcester. I was beginning to contemplate going over myself and collecting her but was aware of the costs that this might incur, and the time it would take. I really wanted Matt to honour the agreement he had made with Kenneth. I needn't have worried however because within a couple of weeks of Matt's attack he was on the phone again saying that he had made the necessary arrangements and would be over with the boat on Saturday, June 21st.

The day dawned and I had borrowed the ORS trailer to pick up the boat. The fact was I didn't have a trailer since selling 'The Spirit of Worcestershire', and Matt had his own that he wanted to take back to Peel to use with the boat he was building. He had had to withdraw from the race but his intention was to sell the part-built craft with the trailer to cut his losses. This made the boat delivery a little more complicated as not only had I to borrow a trailer but also find a means of transferring the boat from one to the other. Normally a forklift truck would do the job but despite my efforts I was unable to find one for the purpose. So it was time to implement plan B!

I decided the best way to do the job was to contact the County Council Sailing Centre at Upton Warren, about 10 miles from Worcester, and ask if I could use their slipway to launch the boat off Matt's trailer and bring her back onto the one I had borrowed. The Centre's staff happily obliged. Matt and his brother duly arrived as arranged on the Saturday. The transfer went smoothly but I was somewhat concerned when I saw the state of the main deck that now had a large hole in it! Matt was very apologetic as he explained to me that they had taken the boat out of the harbour to dispose of the plastic sacks full of gravel they used as ballast. Whilst taking one out of the hold he or his rowing partner had dropped it and it went through the deck! He said he would pay for the materials needed to repair it, but my immediate concern was the fact that I would probably have to replace the whole central deck section which would mean even more time to complete the work. I later heard that the damage had not been sustained by the ballast accident but by a much more malicious and wilful attack on the boat resulting from a dispute over Matt's withdrawal from the race. I never did get to the bottom of this rumour but the fact remained that there was a great deal of work to do on the boat and I needed to get going as soon as possible, as July was only just around the corner and I had to finish the re-fit in time to ship her to the Canaries in December.

So it was with a real sense of anticipation that I brought the boat to the River School in Fernhill Heath, on the edge of Worcester, where my good friend Graham Coyle was Head Teacher. He had lent his support to the project by making a corner of the car park available for the boat, where I was able to rig the adjacent trees with rope and construct a makeshift tent with blue plastic sheets. In the end, after some effort, I created a very serviceable plastic 'boathouse' that enabled me to work on the boat in all weathers, which gave me a great sense of satisfaction. After all the effort since my return at the end of 2001, I now had a boat and was ready to begin the work that would bring her back to a suitable condition for the huge challenge that lay ahead.

The boat just after arrival in Worcester from the Isle of Man and awaiting re-fit by the author.

Chapter Fifteen

It's a bit like waiting for a bus, you hang around for hours and then two come at once! The Saturday after my boat arrived at Upton Warren from the Isle of Man, Louis's boat arrived in Portsmouth, having been shipped from Jersey after he and Kerry had closed the deal.

Louis had asked me if I would be happy to collect her from the docks, so I set out early on Saturday, June 28th, with a borrowed Land Rover. I had an uneventful trip with one stop for a full English! I guess the things that make life worth living are as varied as the people on the planet. The occasional indulgence doesn't do you any harm and for me, setting off at the crack of dawn and covering a reasonable distance, a stop for a large and satisfying breakfast is one of life's little pleasures!

I arrived in Portsmouth and had no trouble finding the right location. I sorted out the necessary paperwork and was told to go out into the yard where the forklift driver would move the boat and trailer from its storage place to the back of my vehicle. I knew these guys shifted stuff all day every day but my heart rate increased when I saw Louis's boat rising heavenward, trailer and all, to a height of some 20 feet before it started to move across the yard with a certain swaying motion that did not inspire huge confidence in me. After a short moment of prayer she began to descend until she came to rest abaft the Land Rover where we eventually managed to attach the rather decrepit trailer to the hitch and begin the journey back to Worcester.

I had decided on the return leg of the journey to call in at a local chandlery and purchase parts and equipment to refit my boat. I drove to the store and spent the rest of the morning ticking off items from the list. I had been in contact with them prior to my visit and asked if they would be happy to give me a discount, but when I got there the person I had been told to talk to did not appear to have any knowledge of the email contact that preceded my visit (could this have been yet another attack of 'potential sponsors memory loss syndrome?). Anyway the list amounted to about £700 and they gave me a rather paltry 10%, every little helps but when you consider the mark up on chandlery products it did seem a little stingy. Still I guess, in fairness to them, they stood to receive no benefit from any help they gave me so I had the satisfaction of adding the final sum to my steadily accumulating debt!

I arrived back in Worcester and parked Louis's boat next to mine on the River School car park to await Louis's return to the UK and his first visit to the boat that would soon dominate his every waking hour.

The race was now on to bring my boat back to a seaworthy state but on the July 12th, my Father died at the age of 91 after a long deterioration brought on by Alzheimer's disease. The conclusion to life eventually comes to us all; in fact it is the only inevitability we all share in common after birth. The way this happens and its effect on those left behind are many and varied and influenced a great deal by the relationships we had with the deceased during their lifetime. In my case I could not have wished for a more concerned and caring Dad, even though work dominated his life and this gave him a certain distance when it came to our family relationship. The fact was that whilst he loved his work, and was therefore very committed to it, he also loved us very deeply and this hard graft was his way of expressing that love. As I grew older I came to realise this more and more and it was with great sadness that we had to endure the inevitable deterioration that this horrible affliction brings. It was even worse for my Mum who cared for him night and day until the final few weeks of his life when she was forced to have him admitted to a care home, as he was becoming to much for her to cope with. Dad's funeral was held at Bessells Green Baptist Church and he was buried alongside other members of our family at St Martin's Church in Brasted, the same location as my christening and later marriage to Usha back in 1977. Its nice to have roots and these kind of connections, history, has a lot to do with the present and much of what we are today seems to rest on all our yesterdays. At the funeral I volunteered to write a tribute to Dad, which was a pretty hard challenge to the emotions when the moment came to read it to the assembled congregation, but I was very glad I had as it all seemed to help with what they call 'closure'.

After we buried Dad I decided to dedicate the forthcoming row to his memory and posted this on the website. Dad would have been hugely proud of my achievement and it seemed fitting to pay tribute to his Fatherhood, the key part he played in the person I am today and the influence that had on my ability to achieve in a variety of facets of my life, including the challenge of the ocean. Here is that tribute which I am proud to share with you as a way of saying thanks to Dad:

Dad born 91 years ago, was most often described as a real gentleman and I guess that sums up the kind of person he was but he was also fun, had a great sense of humour, was hard working and would always go the extra mile for anyone who needed his help.

He was well known and respected within the community of Brasted and lived up the Chart where, shortly after the war, he and other members of both sides of the family built April Cottage, Quiddington and the 'family seat', his beloved Pinehurst, which on completion made the front page of the local paper, a truly grand design long before self build became de rigor.

Dad was also a very discerning chap the most notable example of this trait being his marriage to Margaret in 1948 She became my Mum when I entered the world in 1956, Andrew my elder brother beat me by two years and Alison followed two years later. I know Andrew and Ali would agree they made fine parents and we are proud to have been able to call them Mum and Dad.

As we grew up we came to know and love Dad more and more which also meant we got to hear THOSE stories on many occasions, as well as becoming familiar with his many sayings and idiosyncrasies.

Let me recount just a few, I know Dad would find the following quite amusing:

Dad had a great sense of justice and fair play, he was not at all happy with people who broke the law or took advantage of others, perhaps our political masters should have taken heed of Dad's answer to the problem, as on many occasions after a news bulletin about the latest law breaker, Dad, with reference to some isolated Scottish Island where top-secret tests had been carried out many years ago, would be heard to cry….. "send him to the Anthrax island."

He often thought the law was a bit of an ass and felt that the bible had more of an answer, or at least his interpretation of it. We tried to convince him on a number of occasions that…. "turn the other cheek and bash em" wasn't actually a direct quote from the scriptures but he remained unconvinced!

On that slightly military note, Dad was always a great enthusiast for his days in the Army when he served with the Royal Engineers, he would often talk about his experiences particularly during the Second World War. A chap nick named Big Bang Bailey seemed to have made a great impression on him, which had something to do with the slightly irresponsible use of high explosives, fortunately he survived which was a great blessing from my perspective!

He carried on this military facet to his life, which also turned into service to the community, especially young people, by his long association with the Army Cadet Force. He gave countless hours of voluntary service to this organisation.

Dad was generally very even tempered, mild mannered and I can't remember ever hearing him use any bad language, "oh blast" was about as bad as it got but sometimes when he got really exasperated you would hear his own very unique utterance… "oh Bless the Pope!" one wonders if the Pope will notice the difference now Dad is no longer with us.

Dad worked very hard, it was one of the ways he expressed his love for his family. He felt a real duty to provide for us and this was done through a long association as an employee of the Greater London Council as well as building his own private practice, which filled most of his waking hours. Dad has many memorials to his industrious life and you don't have to travel far around the local area without seeing some building or other that was subject to Dad's attention. The Bible says, " in my Father's house there are many mansions, can I be so bold as to suggest that as of 12th July a lot of them will soon have extensions!

Dad's gracious attitude spilled over into the work place, he would often refrain from giving a builder on one of his jobs an ear bending for poor workmanship or even ignorance as to how to do the job properly and instead would point out the problem and suggest how it might be done to his exacting standards. On occasions this would even mean picking up the shovel and showing the individual how to do the job in such a way that he would gain respect rather than resentment. Dad's building advice touched many members of our extended family and even extended into continental Europe.

Just over a year ago I spent a week looking after Dad whilst Mum took a break from the 24 hour care he needed by this time. In retrospect I really appreciated this opportunity to give something back to Dad. The wacky world of Altziemers is not something I would wish on anyone but Mum is an exceptional person and faced it with fortitude, I know Dad would be the first to give her praise for a job well done. She has cared for many old and infirm relatives and friends and often seen them right through to the end. However Dad was by far the most difficult not only because of the physical and mental deterioration over a long period but also because of the experience of seeing the person you had spent a lifetime with slowly slipping away from you. Mum drove herself to exhaustion and there are few here today that will ever appreciate just how demanding 24-hour care can be. I think Mum's faith and the support of many people helped a great deal during the final months of Dad's life.

To do justice to Dad's life, the person he was and the things he achieved would take a great deal more than these brief moments but Dad's whole philosophy of life can be summed up in his best know quote namely;

"It's a sad heart what never rejoices"!

And to underline this I'll end with a short verse that he oft times quoted:

It's easy enough to be pleasant
When life goes along like a song
But the man worthwhile, is the man with a smile
When everything goes dead wrong!

Sir Ernest Shackleton is someone I have always admired and he once said of life:

"Some people say it is wrong to regard life as a game; I don't think so. Life to me means the greatest of all games. The danger lies in treating it as a trivial game, a game to be taken lightly, and a game in which the rules don't matter much. The rules matter a great deal. The game has to be played fairly, or it is no game at all. And even to win the game is not the chief end. The chief end is to win it honourably and splendidly. To this end several things are necessary. Loyalty is one. Discipline is another. And chivalry is another."

This quote sums up my Dad and the legacy he left me. The view we have on life is often the result of the influence, for good or bad, of those who have been pivotal to our development. I think Dad taught me by example that the value gained by the things we do in life result more from the way we achieve them than what we have actually accomplished. Integrity is a hugely valuable thing and if we lack it we are sourly impoverished. To row an ocean is an awesome achievement but to do it with a lack of integrity can only conspire to de-value that achievement and degrade you as an individual. The greatest thing Dad left me was his integrity, something I find hard to live up to, but it still remains of immense value, particularly in a world where a lot of what he stood for would be considered old fashioned. The kind of traits Shackleton identifies and Dad displayed could now be considered old fashioned but an old master lying out of view and gathering dust doesn't necessarily mean its lost its value, in fact the opposite is probably true.

Dad (1912-2003). Clearing the ground to begin his self-build dream.

On my return to Worcester, work on the boat started in earnest. One of the first jobs was to take off all the old branding, which was done by using a hot air gun to soften the plastic stickers so they could be peeled off easily. When it came to stripping the old boat name from the bow it suddenly struck me that I hadn't given much thought as to what to name the boat for the row. Usha and I talked quite a lot about this and one day I suddenly remembered a boat I had sailed back in the old Ocean Youth Club days called 'Mjojo'. Using this for my inspiration I had the bright idea of naming her after my children Nayna, John and Joshua, using the first two letters of each name. We both thought this was a great choice as it gave the boat a special personal edge. People who go to sea often say how they develop a special relationship with their boat and this would be reflected in the special relationship I already had with my wonderful kids! So 'NaJoJo' it was!

The boat's name was inspired by the author's children.

Initially, the main task was to repair the main deck and set up a new rowing position designed for the solo row. Teddy Rezvoy who had the boat before me had kept the original double configuration, but this had the aft footrest taking up a lot of the space in the well in front of the cabin hatch and I felt this had the potential to catch your leg which might have led to serious injury and didn't make the best use of the well space for cooking and other domestic uses. That aside the damage sustained on deck meant a complete overhaul of the rowing gear, laying of a new centre section and the replacement of both central hatches. Once this had been achieved I moved the rowing position and gear forward.

In the midst of all this activity I had a call from Kenneth asking if I could take the boat across to the company in Newark that was going to ship the boats for the ORS. For a long time it had been accepted that it was only possible to ship one boat at a time in a 40-foot container. Andrew Morris at PA Freight had taken up the challenge and believed he could come up with a solution to fit two boats into one container bow to bow. Sam Knight a fellow solo rower in the 2004 Regatta lived in Newark and so his boat was already available for a trial run at Andrew's solution but a second boat was needed to test his theory, so I set off on Friday, August 15th, towing the boat behind a rather nice Shogun Sport 2.5 TD I had hired in Worcester.

I arrived fairly early in the morning after an uneventful trip and was joined by Kenneth and Sam. We watched as the two boats were loaded onto the wooden sledges PA Freight had constructed and then slowly slid into a 40-foot container Andrew had purchased especially for the job. Sam's boat went in first with inches to spare and from this we ascertained that the sledges fitted almost exactly, but the real test of his theory was about to begin. The first boat's bow was facing the container doors and my boat was about to be pushed in bow to bow. Slowly but surely the two craft came together as the sledges interlocked. The forklift truck kept pushing and the boat kept moving forward until there were only a few inches of the stern left protruding from the container doors. Everyone held their breath, as these last few inches were critical to the success of the idea and consequently the whole shipping process. After a final shove 'NaJoJo' seemed to be just inside but nothing was certain until the doors had been secured properly. Andrew got off the forklift and with millimetres to spare shut the doors to a relieved round of applause and woops of delight. His idea had proved possible but it would turn out to be more of a challenge than expected as the boats turned up later in the year for shipment to the start and back again after the finish. There is no such thing as a standard ocean rowing boat and the variations in design of the keel and set up of the rowing gates would make the whole logistics process less than simple. Once the boats were delivered on the outward journey in Santa Cruz or Bridgetown docks for the return journey to the UK, the sledge design posed an intellectual problem that seemed a bit too challenging for the average wharfy. In Santa Cruz, after the boat had been unloaded, the dockers broke up the sledge and sent the wood back to PA Freight with a bill for their trouble! The idea was to keep the sledges intact for future use and stack them in one container for the trip back to the UK or over to the Caribbean! Anyway the basic principle was sound and in future the loading and discharge probably needs supervising by someone who knows what they are up to and can 'gently persuade' the dock staff how best to tackle the problem!

Work continued relentlessly on the re-fit interspersed with the occasional ORS event like our stand at the Southampton Boat Show over the week of September 12th – 21st. I had been in touch with Dr Mike Duke to ask if he could help once again with the electrics and a new solar array. He was happy to get involved, but was unavailable due to existing work commitments and the next race in Australia for the solar car they were building at the University.

He kindly put me in touch with another solar expert called Paul McGonagle and supplied a number of parts for him to use. Paul came over to do a survey on the boat after I had stripped out the old electrics. He made another couple of trips after that to install the new solar array and wire in the new equipment I had assembled over the previous months. We replaced the old and inefficient panels on the cabin roof that had been there since the boat was built back in 1997, but left the two smaller panels on the bow section which were still operating reasonably well and would act as a top up for the main supply. The two new panels were very impressive being not much thicker than a credit card and producing loads of power that would be quite adequate for all my needs on the crossing. These panels were fixed to the coach roof with marine adhesive and my experience dictates that having panels on frames that you can move towards the sun is totally unnecessary these days with the advances in solar technology. In fact my array weighed hardly anything in comparison to previous set ups, giving a weight advantage and making the boat safer in the event of capsize. In future if ocean rowing race organisers want to achieve a true standard design boat one area that should be looked at is solar arrays. In my opinion any sort of rigid panel on moveable frames should be outlawed, as they are totally unnecessary as solar technology improves and the only real advantage they could give is as a wind scoop thus helping the propulsion of the boat through the water. The argument as to whether or not this gives boats rigged in this manner an unfair advantage will no doubt continue as long as they exist but for any new builds to standard racing designs the arguments stop with new technology at the boat builders yard!

'Najojo', re-fit complete and awaiting shipping.

Paul did a magnificent job that represented the last major task of the refit. I took the boat across to Upton Warren Sailing Centre to test everything on the water. This was the only time I was actually able to do any sort of trial, as time had been so tight. However everything functioned well and I felt confident that we were as ready as we could be for the immense task that lay ahead.

The last job that needed doing required some help, so I appealed in the press for a sign writing company to brand the boat with various logos and web addresses. I had no significant sponsorship but wanted to give the Ocean Rowing Society and my own ocean rower website prominence, plus one or two other things like the boat's name.

Mike Lapac, who owns Universal Display Ltd in Worcester, had part of his business trading under the name 'Signworx'. He rang me and offered his team's services in exchange for their logos on the boat. I accepted this generous offer and Mike's people did a great job. 'Najojo' was finally looking respeldent and ready to leave the UK and go to sea!

On Friday, December 12th, I set off once again for Newark with a fully fitted and equipped boat in tow. The only thing missing was the major part of my food supply that was due to be delivered in La Gomera. I said a fond farewell to 'NaJoJo' at PA Freight and returned home to celebrate Christmas without a boat to distract my attention. It would not be long before I would be saying goodbye and heading off to begin the ultimate challenge of my life so far.

Chapter Sixteen

It was a little bit strange being back on La Gomera, after all, the last time I was here I had just been plucked from the briny deep by Doug and Anita. In a funny sort of way it was good to be back although I felt lousy after what seemed a very long flight from the UK. Usha and I had decided she and the family would stay at home and we would say our fond farewells in Worcester. One of the lessons learnt from the 2001 experience was the trauma of goodbyes on the dock was best avoided! My Mum, who had been staying with us, took me to London where I caught a tube to the ORS and stayed overnight with Kenneth and Tatiana. Kenneth and I rose fairly early the next morning and made our way to Heathrow, thinking we had plenty of time to check in and enjoy the delights of KFC's special privileges in the frequent flyers lounge, or some such indulgence a mere mortal like me had never experienced before. Unfortunately when we finally got there the check in was just closing, our late arrival resulting from an incorrect itinerary given us by the airline! Their schedule should have allowed us at least an hour to spare but as it was we only just had enough time to get to the gate and board. We may not have made it at all but for Kenneth's unique style of getting things done! We got to the end of a long queue for security checks, Kenneth undid the barrier and in his usual stentorian way announced to the assembled and somewhat bewildered onlookers that our flight was about to leave so would they mind us queue jumping. The fact that the request had only been completed by the time we reached the front of the queue didn't seem to worry Kenneth or anyone else as by this time a visible sense of shock had descended upon all present! Being a true Brit I was wishing the ground would open up at this point and swallow me! However we were making good progress to the gate, a fact Kenneth dutifully acknowledged by turning to shout his thanks to half the terminal building as we hurried on!

Getting onto the plane was somewhat of a relief in more ways than one. The most notable event of the flight out was our descent into Tenerife South where the summit of El Tiede, Tenerife's home grow volcano and the highest point in Spain, stood above the cloud cover like a mysterious dark island in an endless white sea. On arrival we went to the baggage claim to find that one of our suitcases was missing. It's a pretty normal occurrence for the international traveller these days, the mind can only boggle at the amount it must cost the airlines to subsequently transport each bag to its destination. Kenneth decided to stay behind at the airport and wait for Peter Hogden, the safety yacht skipper, who was due in on the next flight whilst

I hailed a taxi to take me the short hop to Los Christianos and Fred Olsen's, La Gomera Sea Cat. Los Christianos is the sort of place you want to go through as quickly as possible, unless you are the kind of Brit who only wants to go abroad and find somewhere you can eat chips with every greasy thing that is guaranteed to escort you to an early grave, drink yourself stupid to the sound of very load music whilst avoiding contact with any of those 'Johnny Foreigners' who live on the island! Not my idea of fun but each to his own I suppose. The delights of La Gomera are far more appealing as the island has been largely unspoilt by the ravages of budget tourism. By the time I had boarded the sea cat my head was pounding and I spent most of the 40 minute crossing to San Sebastian with my eyes closed in a reclining seat. On arrival I was met by Louis Ginglo and a few of the other guys who took me to the apartment I would share with Louis for the next week and-a-half before his wife Ellie joined him for the Regatta start, at which point I was destined to repair to 'NaJoJo', that is of course if she had arrived by then (the boat that is not Ellie!). Once I had settled in we went for a walk and it transpired that apart from Samson Knight's boat and that belonging to Sarah and Sally Kettle, which had been there since retirement from the Woodvale Race the previous October, no other boats had yet arrived from Santa Cruz.

Whatever! I was too wrecked after the journey to be all that bothered and Louis and I headed for a local Chinese restaurant for some food that I didn't really enjoy as I was too tired to care and my head still felt like someone was breaking rocks inside. I returned to the flat for an early night. Things would probably look a whole lot better in the morning. Funnily enough this was one of the worst evenings of the whole trip and was the nearest I came to feeling homesick, rather ironic when you think of what lay ahead.

I arrived on the island on Tuesday, January 6th, 2004. The start was scheduled for the 20th and the next couple of weeks were a busy round of preparation for our impending departure. The next day boats slowly began to roll off a succession of sea cat arrivals, generally two a day with Kenneth doing his best to ensure their safe delivery, ably assisted by a band of Eastern Europeans related in various ways to Tatiana. Unfortunately the quality of the trailers they had access to was less than ideal and a number of the boats sustained some damage in transit from Santa Cruz. Kenneth subsequently arranged for a guy from Tenerife to come over a make repairs, so ultimately all the boats were sorted, but it's just a shame they were damaged in the first place. Having said that the same thing happened but for different reasons in Playa San Juan on Tenerife before the start of the 2001 race; some boats were holed when the crane operator dropped them onto trailers in his legendary cack handed manner!

In the end I was boatless for a week, which meant I made myself available to help out were I could with other people's preparations. I ended up cooking for Louis who may well have starved had I not volunteered, so intense were his single minded preparations for the race start, not to mention Ellie's expected arrival! Word spread about the delights of my cuisine as the week advanced and by the following weekend 'Rich's Bistro' was producing meals for a very select little band of rowers and support crew including John Peck, Fraser Dodds, Bob Barnsley, our legendary scrutineer, and Vasilly Galencov, the mad Russian photographer! I ate out quite a lot with Kenneth, Tatiana, and an increasing number of veteran ocean rowers, who proved to be great company and which I enjoyed very much.

Down at the marina more rowing boats were arriving daily. There had been a little decention in the camp due to the lack of all 13 boats being available when the crews arrived but public holidays caused delays that could not have been avoided, especially as the Christmas break was only just over creating a back log of all cargos discharged at Santa Cruz. The atmosphere amongst the rowers, support staff and guests was pretty good, however, and there was a general feeling that everyone was doing their best under sometimes difficult circumstances. Peter Hogden was busy preparing his boat 'Kilcullen' with his two-crew members, Phil and Johan, she would supply safety cover for the race. They were moored alongside Diana and Stein Hoff's catamaran 'White Admiral' with Stein's mum Eli making up the crew. The Hoffs are both veteran ocean rowers and they were also providing some safety cover as well as hospitality, support and training for anyone who wanted their help prior to the start. This included the provision of a daily cold buffet lunch on board 'White Admiral' that became a focal point for the rowers and support team escaping for a welcome break from the heat of the day and the multitude of jobs that needed to be completed before everyone was satisfied that they were ready for sea.

Skipper Peter Hogden preparing our safety vessel, 'Kilcullen', for sea.

Each boat had a thorough inspection by Bob Barnsley, our ORS scrutineer, with everyone greatly appreciating his highly professional but very good natured approach to the task. His scrutiny would sometimes reveal health and safety issues that needed immediate attention, the announcement of which to already stressed crews had the potential for some conflict. However, Bob's diplomatic approach and considerable back up from people like Stein, Diana, Kenneth, veteran rowers and a host of others, along with a large dollop of good humour made light of much of the important work that needed doing and enabled it to be done with good natured speed and efficiency.

'Najojo' arrives at the mooring a week after the author.

I think I was the second boat to be inspected and I didn't have a great deal that needed doing. My main concern was the rudder and finding a way to secure it so it didn't release itself from its brackets in heavy weather. Eventually a solution was achieved by attaching a small block of wood above the two fixing points, which seemed to do the trick. The rudder and steering gear had been exercising my mind on and off during the preceding months of preparation but I felt I had finally resolved the issue as best I could, a point underlined by the successful completion of a few trial runs off the island in subsequent days.

I remember at the start of the 2001 race having certain doubts about our communications equipment and by now you know the story behind what happened with that. The steering gear had not caused me nearly as much anxiety but there remained a hint of a question at the back of my mind about this issue, which it may have been wise to have paid more attention to in the light of events that were to unfold some weeks later.

It appears to me from studying a number of expeditions and challenges that immaculate preparation is the real key to success, or at least to be as successful as you can without considering external factors that you have no control over. In the final analysis, if you have the slightest doubt about a piece of equipment or strategy you are undertaking then it really needs to be sorted before you embark. Running out of time or resources is no excuse for a lack of belief in your ability or equipment. It is better to postpone your start and get it right than delay and miss your window of opportunity to undertake the row in the best possible weather conditions. Late starts are a regular occurrence on the North Atlantic run which only has a brief weather window, roughly between May and September. It seems almost inevitable that rowers planning this trip end up with the boat being delayed in one way or another, final preparations taking longer than expected or their start delayed because of local weather conditions. Even when delays happen, though, people still go and then get rescued or even pay the ultimate price. The North Atlantic on the UK side is best avoided as September draws to a close. So strict deadlines, good preparation, some contingency for delays and the courage to re-appraise the plan are all vital elements to take into consideration. Or better still, work a bit harder and give yourself more time to prepare before hand whilst aiming for realistic goals. Those few extra hours or even days of preparation could save your life once you have begun your challenge!

The couple of weeks on La Gomera prior to the row were reasonably relaxed and enjoyable. Most evenings were spent in the company of other team members, veteran rowers or supporters and the days were filled with all sorts of jobs that needed doing on the boats, stowing gear and generally preparing for what lay ahead. By January 18th, most of what needed doing had been done and in the evening about 100 people assembled at the Club Nautica for the ORS farewell dinner. It was an excellent evening with much good humour, albeit laced with a hint of anxiety. The challenge facing us was looming large on the horizon and within the next 48 hours we would be at sea. Six of us would have the added pressure of entering one of the world's most hostile environments alone!

Monday, January 19th, 2004, was our last full day before the start. San Sebastian had been having its annual Fiesta celebrating its patron Saint. There had been lots of load music well into the early hours of the morning but I had slept reasonably well on 'NaJoJo' as I had left the flat to make way for Ellie's arrival. I got up early and decided it would be nice to get away from the town and all things rowing for a few hours. I decided to see if I could get to the Temperate Rain Forest on the upper reaches of the island. A visit to the Garajonay National Park is one of the highlights of any trip to La Gomera and it appealed to me as pre race 'get away from it all' therapy!

ORS farewell dinner, January 18th, 2004.

Kenneth & my fellow rowers.

I walked out of San Sebastian on the main road that steadily climbs out of the town up into the mountains of the central region. It was very quiet with only the occasional vehicle. I hadn't had any breakfast and only carried a small quantity of water to refresh me on the climb. The views from the road were wonderful and the road itself was quite interesting. The old route had been cut into the steep sides of the hills but in more recent times the biggest and most severe bends had been straightened out with tunnels driven through the rock. I suspect the EU probably funded this. Concrete blocks had been laid across the entrance and exit to the old bends by each tunnel entrance but there was still pedestrian access so I took the longer route round the old road. This was strewn with rocks of various sizes that had fallen from the shear faces above, although many more had gone over the edge and on down into the steep sided ravines below. The extent of this debris caused you to keep a weather eye open in case one should decide to make contact with your head! After several miles I came to what seemed a deserted roadside café, more a sort of shed with tables and chairs outside. I thought I'd see if I could get something that might remotely resemble breakfast and eventually went inside and located a lady behind the counter who spoke as much English as I did Spanish! The end result was a sandwich made from French stick with goat's cheese inside but no butter. It was very tasty but a bit dry. I washed it down with a cup of coffee as I sat at one of the roadside tables with a couple of cats trying to share it with me.

The spectacular interior of La Gomera.

I continued onward and upward until I came to the highest point where the road went into a big tunnel with no pavement. I could see the other end but there was no light inside and it was long enough to be rather hazardous for a pedestrian. In fact I don't think walkers had ever been considered when it was constructed, as it was probably assumed that they would use one of the many footpaths that criss-cross the island. I knew nothing of these and had no time to find them so I decided to take my life into my own hands and leg it through the tunnel. There wasn't much traffic about otherwise I would not have done this as it would have been far too dangerous. I had decided on a zigzag strategy, in other words if a vehicle entered the tunnel at either end I would immediately cross to the other side to give me the best chance of survival! As I entered the tunnel a coach followed me in on the other side of the road its horn blasting with loud contempt at my audacity in even contemplating this reckless strategy. As luck would have it only one other car came through as I ran the full length of the tunnel. I eventually emerged at the other end with my heart pounding at a rate far in excess of the effort of running such a distance under normal circumstances. In retrospect my own evaluation of this action drew me to the conclusion that it was rather idiotic but did stem from the apparent lack of any other obvious way of getting to the Park on foot, apart from a Chris Bonnington type expedition over the mountain peak the tunnel passed under.

I was rewarded with a magnificent view on the other side but then started having a personal debate as to where I should go next. There were no signposts and I was beginning to consider how I might eventually get back to San Sebastian, as I didn't fancy doing the tunnel run for a second time. I was very high and the road dropped away to my left, twisting out of sight along the mountain contours then appearing again as it meandered steadily and steeply downwards along the side of one of the many deep ravine that spread out like the spokes of a wheel from the centre of the island to the coast.

Such is the inaccessibility of the island's geography that the locals, in years gone by, had measured distance by the time and effort necessary to hike the paths rather than the number of miles between two places which was never all that far. The trip from one ridge to another down a steep ravine and up the other side could take the weary traveller several hours, even though the straight line distance may only have been a few hundred metres. To combat the topography and save hours of time and effort the locals developed the Gomeran Whistle, a special form of communication originating in pre-Hispanic times. It did not constitute a language in the strict sense of the word but a form of 'speech' that spells out syllables by means of a whistle with the help of fingers inserted into the mouth, a sort of musical Morse Code! As the rural society that used this language has disappeared and other means of communication such as the telephone have been introduced, the Gomeran Whistle is scarcely used, meaning that fewer and fewer people nowadays can practice the art.

Anyway my immediate problem was what I should do next. Far out of 'whistle shot' and a long way down the twisty mountain road was a small village. I thought I might attempt to reach it and perhaps find a bus or taxi that could eventually take me back to San Sebastian, but it was a few miles away across the ravine and whilst the decent would not be a problem the climb back up, plus the 12 miles back to the Marina should no transport be available, was starting to worry me. It was a beautiful day, however, and the scenery was spectacular, so I decided to press on.

As I turned yet another sharp bend in the road I was confronted with a large sign in the apex of the main road and another route, which forked left and began to climb steeply upwards, whilst the road I was on continued its manic decent. To my surprise and pleasure the sign marked the boundary of the PARQUE NACIONAL DE GARAJONAY. I had reached my destination almost by accident and now stood at the foot of a considerable ascent on a road that snaked up the mountainside in a seemingly endless series of hairpin bends. It was a long way to the top, but I began the climb in positive mood having 'discovered' the park for myself whilst enjoying the natural splendour of this beautiful island.

The climb went on and on. I was aware that time was also ticking by and I really needed to be thinking about getting back to the boat. I guess I had covered between 12 and 15 miles, the majority uphill since starting early in the morning. I had reached the edge of the Park and walked up into the temperate rain forest that it is famous for, so felt that I had achieved what I set out to do even though I sensed there was a huge amount more to see given more time. I guess it had been there for tens of thousands of years, so it could wait to reveal more of its hidden secrets when I return to the island on a future visit.

I turned and began to walk back down the road thumbing a lift from the occasional, disinterested, motorist. Eventually an empty taxi came up and stopped beside me. The driver must have deposited his fare at the top of the mountain and was heading back to San Sebastian. He pulled up and asked if I wanted a ride but made sure I was clear that this was as a paying customer and not a hitchhiker. I was glad to see him and had no problem with the payment because at least it would mean that I would return through the tunnel safely and might even make the start of the Regatta in one piece! I was back at the Marina in time for a late lunch on 'White Admiral' where I recounted the delights of the morning's stroll and the wonderful experience I had enjoyed.

I walked along the breakwater after lunch in pensive mood. My gaze moved from the sheltered waters of the harbour bay entrance out into the open ocean beyond. I thought about the highs and lows of the last 6 years, the hours and hours of preparation for the first row, the cost of the commitment and the ultimate failure that had spurred me on to the point in my life where I now stood lost in the magnitude of it all. I thought about all the incredible people I had met who had become an integral part of my life, not least my awesome wife and brilliant children who had supported me all the way through this crazy enterprise. I would bear their names on the boat when I rowed out into the unknown the following day. I wasn't frightened or worried, in fact I felt as prepared as I would ever be for what lay ahead and was looking forward to leaving. I had very little comprehension of what life on the open ocean would be like in such a small craft but knew that if the ocean were gracious enough to let me pass then I would make it to the other side.

Chapter Seventeen

Iwoke early on Tuesday, January 20th, 2004, with the inspirational words of Sir Winston Churchill, spoken in 1942, occupying my thoughts as I rubbed the sleep from my eyes, climbed out of the cabin and set foot on the pontoon alongside 'NaJoJo': -

Now this is not the end. It is not even the beginning of the end. But it is, perhaps, the end of the beginning.

Those words, I thought, pretty much summed up the stage at which I now found myself.

Tuesday may have seemed an odd day to leave, but one reason we organised the ORS Regatta was to commemorate the first Atlantic Solo row by John Fairfax who departed exactly 35 years before on January 20th, 1969, arriving in Florida 180 days later.

My first objective was to find some breakfast, however, so I walked across the road into town hoping that somewhere would be open for trade. It was very quiet as most of the locals were still sleeping off the effects of the recent festivities. The town square café bar had just shown the first sign of life so I ordered a toasted cheese and bacon sandwich, a poor substitute for the full English I thought I deserved. I sat outside and was joined by one of the double crews and respective female companions. The mood was light, if a little strained, and I wasn't sure whether my presence was welcome or not, given that in a few hours they would be separated for a long and uncertain period; perhaps the opportunity for final fond farewells was more attractive than making polite conversation with the Captain and crew of 'Najojo'!

I finished my coffee and walked back to the boat. There really wasn't much to do but wait. I occupied my time with final checks of gear and equipment whilst chatting to passers by, crewmembers, ORS staff, and the ever-expanding crowd of supporters.

We had received our final briefings and all that was left to do was take the group photo! When I arrived back at the boat I found a couple of glasses of whiskey on deck. I had given Doug and Anita a bottle of single malt as a thank you for all they had done, not only for me but for everyone involved in the Regatta since we took the island by storm a couple of weeks before. They wanted to raise a glass and wish me luck, which was a very kind gesture, and once the toast had been made Anita introduced me to a rather smart teddy bear with a brown ribbon round his neck. He was to become my companion and mascot for the trip and I decided to call him 'Dougan' after my favourite Gomeran couple. The lump in my throat was a sure signal that it was time to cast off and gently row out of the marina into the harbour bay to make ready for the 11 o'clock start. I felt as though stepping off the pontoon and thereby separating myself from land for the final time should be of great significance, but I don't think the enormity of what I was about to undertake had really sunk in (although that may not be the best way to describe it!). It would have been interesting to know how other crews dealt with these final moments before departure, suffice to say the lack of presence of my nearest and dearest was a definite plus, particularly when I cast my mind back to the scenes of our leaving in 2001.

Final photograph of the ocean rowers before the Challenge started.

I picked up one of the two pairs of oars I would use to power my tiny craft across the infinite expanse stretching away from the island and secured one to port and the other to starboard. Other boats were beginning to pull away as purposeful blades ruffled the clear waters of the Marina. I watched John Peck and Fraser Dodds in their boat, 'New Horizons', carefully navigating their way round pontoons as they made their way to the entrance. They soon disappeared into the forest of masts created by maritime residents not quite ready for one reason or another to point their bows towards the open ocean.

The author rows 'Najojo'out of the Marina's safe haven to the start line,
January 20th, 2004.

I patiently waited my turn, when sufficient room would allow me to begin the first of a million strokes that would take me on my way to the Caribbean. It finally arrived; mooring ropes were untied as willing hands pushed 'Najojo' away from the jetty and my final contact with the shore for a very long time. I bent to the oars and as I came round the landward side of the breakwater and into the marina entrance a substantial crowd of spectators and well wishers had assembled to shout their good wishes and encouragement, including a couple not only from Worcester but also customers of Checketts, the butchers in the little village of Ombersley, who had been so supportive of the whole undertaking almost from the beginning back in 1998. "Good luck Richard"! "Take care!" and other such cries of encouragement descended from the harbour wall above, this really was it; I was suddenly aware of the stark contrast that this departure represented compared with the last time I left one of these fascinating islands on a voyage that proved far less of a success than I hoped this one would turn out to be! Leaving La Restinga at night with only three people to wave me goodbye was very different to the many people enjoying the spectacle bathed in the warm Gomeran sunshine. For a brief moment amidst the hustle and bustle of the race start I wondered if I would live to see another Christmas and celebrate it with my family and a traditional Checketts Bronze free-range turkey! I sincerely hoped I would!

A total of 13 boats jostled for position at the start. 'Queensgate' was making a record breaking attempt to be the fastest and first ocean going four ever to put to sea, with Jason Hart (30) Phil Langman (29) Yorkie Lomas (35) and Shaun Barker (25) at the oars.

Six doubles would be in hot pursuit with Sally (26) and Sarah (45) Kettle attempting to be the first trans-Atlantic mother and daughter ocean rowing team. Their boat 'Calderdale-The Yorkshire Challenger' had entered the Woodvale race for double crews the previous year with Sally and her boyfriend on board, but he suffered from epilepsy and could not keep his medication down on account of seasickness so they had to retire. Sally was determined to finish what she set out to do and asked her Mum to come along instead!

Chris Morgan (40) and Michael Perrens (31), both military types from the Parachute Regiment, Chris retired and working on oil rigs whilst Michael was still active within the Regiment, rowing 'Carpe Diem', the old boat belonging to Jan and Dan Meek who succeeded in becoming the first mother and son team to cross the Atlantic in 1997.

William Stableforth (30) and Nathaniel Spring (30) began their oceanic assault aboard 'Sea Slug', whilst 'Linda' carried James Doust and Nigel Gower (38).
John Peck (58) and Fraser Dodds (46) crewed 'New Horizons', one of two boats in the Regatta built for previous ocean going events in the Channel Island of Jersey.

A few weeks before leaving for La Gomera I had driven to the Isle of Ely after delivering 'Najojo' to the shippers in Newark in order to collect 'Kenneth C', crewed by Henry Dale (41) and Justin Coleman (38).

Then there were my fellow solo rowers, all six of us looking forward to many weeks of unknown isolation.

Matthew Boreham had built his quaint little boat in his garage, the dimensions of which had determined the size of the hull! This was Matt's fourth attempt to row an ocean; that says something for his determination to succeed. I think everyone was gunning for everyone else and wished fellow rowers great success but I was particularly hopeful that Matt would win through this time to fulfil his personal ambition.

Pavel Rezvoy (65) from the Ukraine was one of two overseas entries in the Regatta and the oldest of the field. His boat 'Marion Lviv' had a great deal of work to be done when she eventually arrived at the marina, but a committed band of volunteers worked tirelessly to have her ready in time.

Samson Knight (23) represented the other end of the age range in his boat 'Pacific Pete TNT' and Mark Mortimer of 'Acorn Atlantic Warrior' was making a solo attempt after completing a trans-Atlantic double in the 1997 event.

Louis Ginglo (38) crewed 'Moose on the Move', representing Canada, in the other boat whose origins were in Jersey.

Last but far from least was yours truly (47) in 'Najojo'. I pulled at the oars, leaving the marina entrance behind. By this time a varied array of vessels where chumming about the bay waiting for the start. The Hoff's catamaran 'White Admiral' was waiting in a pre-arranged position designed to create an imaginary start line between her and the far end of the harbour wall. The idea was for all of us to get the stern of our boat close in under this wall for 1100 hours, when the Regatta would begin with the sounding of a claxon. To be honest not everyone started from behind the line but I didn't think a few yards here and there would make much difference with nearly 3,000 nautical miles ahead of us!

Rowing is a funny old sport as everything is done backwards! It means you are never quite sure what you may be about to run into, but when you come to depart from somewhere you constantly look back at the view, which is nice. As the seconds ticked away I looked back up the road as it stretched away out of San Sebastian, up into the mountains I had climbed the previous day; it all seemed an awful long time ago and now here I was surrounded by boats and well wishers but somehow strangely alone.

There was great excitement in the air as the final countdown to the start echoed across the water: 10, 9, 8, 7, 6, 5, 4, 3, 2, 1, GO! GO! GO! Not only did the claxon sound a long blast from the start boat but also a cacophony echoed off the rock face behind the marina as boats sounded their hooters, people cheered and then, for a brief moment everything was drowned out by the sound of a maroon exploding over the little town. It seemed like everyone was celebrating the beginning of each individual story that would unfold over the following weeks and months, stories of such epic proportions that no one, especially those whose backs now bent to the oars and faces to the wind, could countenance the enormity thereof.

The weather conditions were perfect. A fresh wind from the North blew over the stern assisting the boat over a short, steep, sea, it felt like nature herself was on our side and enjoying the occasion. I was surprised at how quickly the little port of San Sebastian merged into the greater island landscape, white buildings becoming less well defined and blending into each other the farther out I went. I was rowing along the coast but diagonally away from the island almost due South, giving impressive views of the sun soaked volcanic cliffs that fell steeply into the sea. I had wondered what these initial stages would feel like considering the history stowed in my personal locker. Would the failure of the first attempt be a disadvantage or motivate me to press on no matter what the cost? Right now it all seemed very positive and any skeletons in the locker appeared for the present to belong to Davy Jones! I just hoped this state of mind would continue. I was really enjoying myself as one of the diminishing fleet of vessels that accompanied us from the start drew alongside. I remember Dixie Dean was aboard shooting footage of 'Najojo' and me tackling the initial stages of life at sea, with other familiar faces around him as their owners encouraged me on. Someone suggested I take a different course as many of the other boats had left the island at a much more acute angle, but I'd been here before and had spent many hours, possibly years, planning a strategy. One of the lessons I have learnt in life is to stick to your plans until there is a genuine reason to re-appraise. In fact re-appraisal was a word that would become all too familiar as the journey began to unfold. She soon bore away and began the journey back to San Sebastian. All of a sudden I was alone. Most of the rest of the fleet had slipped from view except for one boat I was passing that was clearly having a great deal of trouble steering a straight course. It was 'Linda' and I knew they had hand steering gear. They were suffering exactly the same problems we had encountered on the 'Spirit of Worcestershire' in 2001. Pulling a line whilst trying to row is just about impossible; by the time you have got the line where you think you want it, and locked it off in a cleat, the boat has succumbed to the prevailing weather conditions and gone broadside on so you have to repeat the process all over again. In the end you go from one side to the other through 180 degrees and end up frustrated and exhausted. It's the pits. In 2001 I vowed that I would never go to sea with a hand steering rig again, except as a possible emergency back up.

I rowed on watching them heading towards the island one minute and back out again the next. Ah well at least I was ahead of at least one of the double crews. Everyone else was now out of sight and I began to turn my attention to exactly what sort of regime I would employ on a daily basis and to other essential items like navigation.

On many occasions before the start we were advised that if you manage to get out of sight of land and through the first couple of weeks of the row in one piece you should make it the rest of the way! Not sure if this can be proven statistically but I know for a fact that the first week is a bit of a watershed for an ocean row. Everything is unfamiliar, if you are prone to seasickness this is probably when you will be laid low, fortunately something I have never suffered from. If your preparations have been less than exemplary, this is probably when you will find out, and if you decided to go with that second hand water maker *et al* because the budget was diminishing too fast, this is when you will realise what a bad decision it was and that it is far too late to do anything about it!

My first week was as predictably unpredictable as any for the would-be ocean rower. To give you an idea of the kind of things one has to face I'll give you exclusive access to my log book. I made log entries as part of my routine every day at 1200 hours local time. During this week I was coming to terms with a hostile environment on an unsteady platform in total isolation apart from the boat's communications equipment. This amounted to a short range hand held VHF only useful for ship to ship contact via line of sight, which was about 2 miles, and a satellite telephone which worked really well but at great cost. It had a free inward text messaging feature and we set up a link on my website so people could text me at regular intervals from their computers in the comfort of their own homes. This facility was a real lifesaver and accessing my text messages became a regular morale-boosting feature of my evening routine. Suffice to say this wasn't much when taken in the context of the huge challenge that lay ahead. On the other hand it was luxury when compared with historic rows before the advent of satellite navigation and communication.

I have read other accounts in the past that concentrate almost exclusively on the content of the ship's logbook or get very nerdy about the technicalities of the challenge. This can get a little tedious so I will endeavour to make this as readable as possible with some serious editing, but with regard to this first seven days I'll re-create the log entries exactly as they were with just a few footnotes as and when necessary. Each entry is a written review of the last 24 hours of progress.

SHIP'S LOG PART 1 OUTWARD

Tuesday January 20ᵗʰ, 2004, 1200 hours.

Off San Sebastian La Gomera.
Departed La Gomera Marina 1100 for race start on schedule. 13 boats finally left 6 solo 6 double 1 four.
Set course due South 120 miles.
Wind from N force 4 good rowing conditions.
1x5.1 kn burst.
Adjusting to life on my own at sea. It has started well. 4 dolphins round boat this evening.
No rowing regime as yet. Slept from 2000 hours on and off until 0400 rowed and at first light made breakfast did about 7 miles on course overnight. This boat's handling is very impressive. Rowed in the morning, made water and sorted a couple of things. Wind gone round to East, bit of a pain, tried to continue my southerly course but sea getting up and no good on beam + poor progress. Decided not to fight it and now going with it but trying to still nibble out some southing. Hope it goes into the North later.

Wednesday Jan 21ˢᵗ, 1200 hours   N27° 33'.185
32 miles   Wind 4-5   W17° 10'.655

First full day at sea. Now running with easterly wind no other option. Making good progress but would prefer if it was South at this stage. Will have to reset route later or tomorrow.

Thursday Jan 22ⁿᵈ, 1200 hours   N27° 22.720
Wind ESE 3-4   32.7 miles   W17° 38.173

Did the same mileage as yesterday but not in the direction I would have preferred. Need to re think route and may ditch first waypoint and go to second. I am several miles off El Hierro at present but to near for comfort I just want to get well away from the Canaries then worry about the rest of the trip. I have come close to a couple of other rowing boats overnight so I know I haven't been left behind! I am praying for Northerly or NE wind but yesterday's East wind is now ESE which is hopeless for getting South. I am not quite sure what happens next but I will look at the charts in a mo. Just need a good strong favourable wind to get me on my way. Apart from that I'm feeling ok Bit tired and not sure my CD Player is usable as the solar battery charger doesn't seem up to the job wish I had installed one off the main rig (stupid boy!) MH food's a bit bland I think I am better having small amounts often. Anyway, getting used to me little home and the environment.

Friday 23rd Jan 1200 GMT   *N27° 11.337*
Wind E 3-4   *26.4 miles   Max Speed 4.9 knts*   *W17° 55.3*

Less mileage last 24 hrs would like to see a higher average. Cleared El Hierro though still in site. Stopped about dusk last night felt lack of motivation and decided to have a good rest. Started on the oars just before sunrise but it was a struggle to get going. Not totally at peace with myself as yet but not in a state! Worried about if I am eating enough things like that but I think given time it should be ok. Saw two ships in the distance last night one big bulk carrier. This morning whilst having breakfast another came past perhaps a couple of miles off (looked close) hope this isn't a shipping lane as I'd like to get away from it. Navigation vs. weather conditions is a bit of a contentious subject. I want to get South but this easterly wind isn't helping. Last night however I woke with the wind behind us in a perfect position and blowing great guns so I shut down and left the boat to it. Quite a change from the calm conditions at the end of the day. Lets hope the next 24 break the 32 mile barrier. Now MH lunch horaah!

Saturday 24th Jan 1200 GMT   *N26° 51.607'*
Wind ESE F4   *39.7 miles   Max 5.9knts*   *W18° 27.854'*

Choppy sea, confused and difficult to row in. Set the boat up last night and she performed very well, I am impressed! Had first rain overnight quite noisy in the cabin but cleaned up the panels. No rowing as almost impossible in this sea and probably would not have made a lot of difference. If anything may have slowed progress! Checked everything in the middle of night and the wind had come round to ESE (*I think this should have read ENE*) rather than E giving me a bit more advantage for the Southerly direction I want to go. Best mileage so far today! Called Ush last night good to chat I am second in solos and mid field overall which is great. Also had 30 text messages which was great. This morning batteries on radio expired which doesn't seem to have lasted long. May be a problem, as the solar charger doesn't seem very efficient. Should have installed a charger off the main system but too late now!! I'll have to try a couple of ideas as I have been enjoying the BBC World Service. Anyway hoping for another good mileage 24 hours now. Just about keeping course.

Sunday Jan 25th, 1200 GMT   *N26° 30'.326*
Wind E F3   *34.6 miles   Max 5.5kts*   *W18° 52'.452*

Spent a very frustrating afternoon yesterday trying to sort out the radio. In the end it appeared to be a combination of the batteries needing a charge and something in the compartment to jam them up a bit. (*Basically the batteries when put into the back of the world band radio did not push hard enough against each other to carry the current so I had to improvise!*) I sent most of the afternoon sorting this out and was hugely frustrated by it, particularly as I didn't row which meant a poor mileage. As it happened the mileage was ok but I'm not sure whether I'll have enough batteries to go all the way with the World Service. So frustrating, should have had Paul put a charger in!! The weather was fairly benign overnight and this a.m. I have been row since 0600 with breakfast, water making and bodily functions between. In good spirits but would like the wind to come round a bit out of the East and get a bit more South but we are doing ok wind at least is not against us.

Monday 26th Jan 1200 GMT   N26° 05'.202
Wind SSE F1-2   34.4 miles   Max4.7kts   W19° 13'.320

Nice surprise to see I have done another 34 miles in the last 24. Thought with the wind decreasing considerably overnight I'd be looking at less (not complaining!) Trouble is the wind is going into the South a bit now, which is bad news. Just want favourable conditions to Waypoint South 2, which will really be No1 as I have had to re-evaluate the course. S@ represents the real departure point for Barbados and completes the getaway from the Canaries bit. Not a lot to report in the last 24, did a mash and fried onion tea last night which was very nice and a change from MH stuff. Found I'd had a gas leak in the cooker which meant I lost some gas, thought I could smell it when I opened the hatch, anyway tightened it all up now so should be ok for rest of trip. Started rowing at sunrise today just before 0800 couldn't manage to get up before that but the average daily rate is ok from my point of view. Should get better as I go South. Turned the phone on last night (no Usha you see!!! Ha ha joke!!!) and it delivered text messages, so you obviously don't have to make a call for them to be delivered. Been rowing and watermaking this a.m. may have a dip soon as its really hot and the cabin gives no real relief. Saw yacht this a.m. thought it was the Hoffs but obviously not as it passed by.

Tuesday 27th Jan 1200 GMT   N25° 50.169
Wind E F1-2   22miles   Max 3.5 kts   W19° 26.523

Well the distance over the last 24 hours speaks for itself, very frustrating. We have had Easterly wind from day two but it has gone round towards ESE & SE over the last 24 hours and last night I was virtually becalmed. You row your guts out but achieve little without the aid of the weather. The prevailing wind should be NE but there has been no sign of anything like that. Anything from NW to NE would be welcome especially around F 4ish, I just want to make some progress!!! Saw a ship on the horizon to the East (again) bulk carrier going South not with the same traction problems as I have got, I guess the others are in the same position except for those way ahead. All I need do now is try and keep my head together. Phoned my first report last night to Ush which was good. Slept well but Oh some favourable weather. I guess at least it's not a head wind!! I'll just have to try and push on as best I can.

Those seven entries cover the first full week at sea. At this stage I hadn't realised the prophetic nature of the unfavourable weather, especially the wind direction as each day took me further into the open ocean. However I had survived the first seven days and covered 221.4 nautical miles, which wasn't spectacular but represented a successful start, especially when considering how this challenge was so outside the orbit of 'normality'.

Chapter Eighteen

It took some time for me to really get to grips with my new environment. Even though I had lived with this project for about seven years, the reality of actually putting to sea and living in such a small space can never truly be prepared for. Regular trips to the gym or time spent working on the boat, even the occasional sea trial in the relative span of time is short lived. On many occasions I would spend whole days in a variety of activities preparing for the row, but there was always room to move and opportunity for change. The irony of this reality is the fact that whilst the vessel designed as your life support system and exclusive means of transportation is so small, the vastness of the environment within which she floats is second only to space itself. A prisoner within eternity or an opportunity to experience something so immense it can take your breath away. Let the mind games begin!

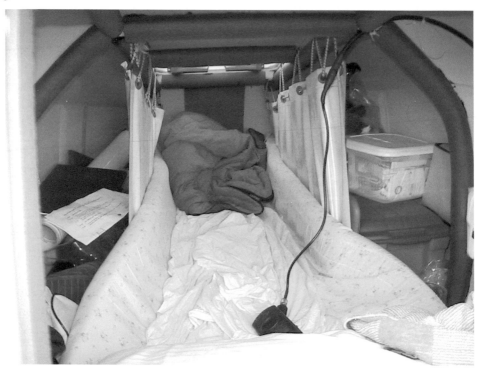

The author's home throughout his epic voyage. Charts and navigational gear on left, bed in middle with sat phone and medical supplies on right.

More and more focus in sport these days is on the psychology of it all, the current wisdom dictates the winner has to be prepared to a peak of mental as well as physical fitness to succeed. Of course this always presumes an understanding of what constitutes winning or success and how such things are determined and by whom. I believe many of the truly astounding feats of human achievement and endurance where individuals and groups have really won through go unrecorded or do not receive the acclaim that they deserve, which constitutes a great loss to the richness of human experience. That is probably the subject of another book but there is no doubt that the ability to survive and succeed in an ocean rowing challenge depends on your mental attitude. I refuse to give way on the need for exemplary preparation at every level of an ocean row, after all it is not only your own life you may put at risk by your actions but once all the equipment is in place and you have reached a high level of physical fitness there may still be a large and terminal hole in your game plan if you lack things like courage, determination, fortitude, patience and the ability to hold it all together when risks need to be taken. How do you prepare for this? To be honest I'm not to sure, there is a huge infra structure being built and loads of money to be made within the psychology of sport but whether or not that can actually change an individual or merely assist one to ultimate success who knows? Perhaps knowing your capabilities and using them to reach your full potential whilst occasionally surprising yourself along the way is what life is all about. So often we loose out because we don't understand what we are really capable of and if we never discover this, can we ever really live life to the full?

January 2004 San Sebastian, La Gomera to N24 05.9' W21 48.8'.

Anyway enough of this philosophising! Suffice to say a great deal of the first week at sea was spent getting my head around the whole thing, even if I didn't realise this at the time. One of the big challenges was to establish a viable routine. This would set the benchmark for progress and until I had put this in place I only had a haphazard series of events strung together to justify my existence. However, routine for its own sake can be as much a hindrance to progress as none at all and my advice to the would-be rower is to go with a range of alternatives in mind and try a bit of experimentation until you find the regime that suits you best at any one particular time. Don't be afraid to change it if circumstances create a new or different situation. Whatever you end up doing will depend on what you are trying to achieve. For example I hardly ever rowed at night but my goal wasn't to win a race, it was to successfully row an ocean. I wanted to do this, as fast as I could and if I won a good placing in the 'competition' as a result so much the better, but that wasn't my motivation so my eventual routine reflected that. Everything was new and different, so establishing myself within this environment concurrently with trying to feel comfortable with it was no mean task.

Routine became a central feature of establishing daily progress and peace of mind; when the routine was disturbed it became more of a mental struggle than just how easy or hard it was to fix the problem that caused the interruption in the first place. For example you may have picked up from my log entries the difficulties that arose during the first week with my CD player and world band radio power supplies or the gas leak on the Sea Cook stove. First of all I had to identify the problem and then set about trying to resolve it, all of which took time. My main focus was on progress, getting to my destination, any hindrance to this primary task needed fixing. The problem with problems is the time and effort they take to resolve and if, in the final analysis, they cannot be resolved more time needs to be spent re-appraising the situation and applying alternative strategies. Coping with such situations are all part of any major challenge but the enormity of the mental struggle these obstacles caused by disturbing the routine and therefore reducing progress was something I found hard to come to terms with. It all came down to mental attitude and as the journey progressed I began to see that mileage wasn't everything, and every day brought new challenges that needed to be addressed positively and seen not necessarily as a hindrance but just another part of the rich tapestry of adventure. It's a tapestry that is probably viewed from the back most of the time you are out there, but when its completed and you turn it over you suddenly realise what a perfect, beautiful and intricate work you have created. Perhaps this gives some understanding as to why people embark on such challenges.

Each week I compiled a report, which I would dictate onto an answer phone and Usha would then type and circulate, via my news group. The local media used these reports to form the basis of regular press articles that enabled the story to unfold at home and give anyone interested some understanding about my life at sea. This strategy proved wonderfully successful and generated a constant stream of text messages each evening to my satellite telephone.

As I sent off the first report on the evening of Monday, January 26th, I was surprised at how quickly the first week had gone. I reflected on how good the start had been with a fair wind taking us South. After only 30 miles, however, it went into the East, thwarting my plan to continue almost due South to avoid El Hierro at all costs and make my first waypoint many miles further down towards the African coast, before striking West for the Caribbean.

Despite the unfavourable weather I reflected on the fact that I had been achieving a daily average of 32 nautical miles and considering I was hauling about three quarters of a ton of boat and equipment over a distance representing more than a marathon a day, I was feeling quite pleased with myself. I was enjoying the spectacle of it all: I had seen dolphins and birds, and, as I left the Canaries further and further behind, the light pollution was replaced by the majesty of the universe. You just don't realise how little of the night sky you normally see on land especially in the UK where you are never far from the incandescent glow of city life. On a clear night in the deep ocean when the moon is not full or has yet to rise, you can see literally billions of stars, it is truly magnificent. I referred to it as the firmament and had several one sided chats with Dougan about the splendour of it all. I rowed throughout every day and into the night during this first week, partly due to the fact that I had no desire to make another unscheduled visit to El Hierro. One thing that did strike me was the comparative ease and speed with which I did eventually clear the islands. The huge bulk of El Hierro was always there to starboard but thankfully the patterns of streetlights from the little towns and villages high up on top of its volcanic mass, so familiar in 2001, remained a distant memory. It made me realise just how much time we had spent in the shadow of the archipelago during that first attempt.

I rowed on into the second week, the start of which was dominated by a total lack of wind and the first becalming of many. On this occasion it was somewhat of a novelty with an oily swell and the intensity of the sun's glare magnified by the surface of the sea, with no hint of any soothing wind to stem the unrelenting heat of the day. This was bad rowing weather and the silence was an intensity I had never experienced before. There is always some kind of noise in normal life and even when I have been up an isolated moor or mountain and been struck by the peace on a calm day it pales into insignificance when compared with the sound of the ocean's silence. It is so quiet it almost hurts and gives some incentive to bend your back to the oars once more with each blade creating miniature vortices that disturb microscopic plankton into a spectacle of jewelled phosphorescence. The sea can be cruel but also very beautiful and the ocean rower is in the privileged position of making his or her way in such a slow and peaceful manner, which in itself brings rewards very few others will ever appreciate. When I worked on cargo ships all those years ago you were always aware of the sea but were somehow separate from it; as an ocean rower I seemed to have become a part of it.

I noted the southerly passage of a bulk carrier on the eastern horizon with some envy regarding her lack of the same 'traction' problems I was experiencing! I took some consolation in the fact that out there somewhere my fellow rowers were probably experiencing the same conditions, or where they? My mind plagued me with unanswerable questions of no real significance, as there was very little I could do about my position even if I had wanted to. I was vaguely encouraged that I wasn't subject to a head wind but from the weather perspective there was little to raise my spirit at this stage of the voyage and, let's face it, I had only just begun!

On Wednesday, January 28th, I took out the Sea Cook stove to prepare lunch and found that the cylinder I had put on the day before was empty! It should have lasted at least a week and I knew there was a problem by the smell of gas I had experienced each time I opened the 'galley locker'. After some investigation I discovered two problems, first of all the valve was leaking, a fact exposed by submerging it under water and watching regular bubbles rising from it even though it was turned off, and secondly the valve control could easily get knocked on when it was stowed after use thus discharging the gas and emptying the cylinder! I was unimpressed as it was a brand new stove, but putting the cylinder on and taking it off each time I used it, resolved both problems even though it was a bit of a pain. I realised I should have brought spare parts for the stove and made a back up plan in case of total failure. Fortunately this new strategy worked for me but the thought of having to eat cold food for several months was less than appealing. Taking a spare would have been a good strategy!

I rowed on despite being greeted by another calm dawn. By evening I was only a few miles from Waypoint 2, at N 25° W 20° (you may remember I was unable to make Waypoint 1 due to the unfavourable wind). I woke at 0400 hours on the morning of January 30th to find that I had been pushed further West than I would have liked, but I made some changes to the boat set up and by the time I started rowing again the wind was from the NE; I noted in the log that "We are on our way AT LAST!!" In the end I decided to strike out towards the Caribbean, seven miles north of Waypoint 1, as there was little need to hit the exact spot. I pointed the bow towards my next Waypoint, Atlantic 1, some 600 nm to the west.

I rowed on with a following wind of force 4-5 to assist me on my way with 10-12 foot waves, some of which were breaking. These conditions were great fun and helped pile on the miles, often giving totals in excess of 40 miles a day. The thing I really began to notice by now was the huge Atlantic swell. Under the seas, whipped up by the prevailing wind, were enormous pulses of energy, very long and wide. They were of no danger to the boat and because of their sheer size looked like great rolling hills. In fact it was only when I had gone over the top of one and looked at it from behind as it sped away to some distant shore did I realise just how big it was and the awesome power that must be locked up in the millions of tons of water it displaced. It is very hard to describe these if you have never experienced them but if you imagine a country scene of low green rolling hills, like those on Salisbury Plain, and think of them moving at considerable speed one after the other without a pause then you might get some idea of what I was experiencing!

I decided to make a change to my daily regime. Up to this point I had rowed fairly consistently from first light at about 0500 to dusk at 1800-1900 hours. From 1100 until 1500 hours the heat became very intense. The idea with the new routine was to avoid this part of the day, and after writing the log at 1200 hours, followed by lunch, I would rest until 1600 and then row on until midnight. I tried this once! Ironically on a day with cloud cover and a breeze to kept things relatively cool! I rowed until 2100 hours and then decided I'd had enough. It was a great idea but didn't suit me so I abandoned it and decided to suffer the heat. To be honest with regular daytime cabin temperatures of 35°C it wasn't very restful anyway, so that was that.

The heat did present a bit of a problem and in the past the media, God bless them, have got very excited about rowers going naked to keep cool and comfortable, but I am of the opinion that such action only results in a human barbeque and decided this wasn't a sensible daytime strategy. For the male rower the combination of free willy and the potential hazard posed by a sliding seat isn't even worth contemplating either! I wore silk long johns and a long sleeved silk tops most of the time during the day to protect myself from the sun's intensity. As the heat increased the further West we went I'd soak these garments in a little fresh water before putting them on which helped to keep me cool even though they dried out pretty fast.

The skin cancer risk was something else I vaguely contemplated at times, especially when I discovered a round red patch on my left foot that didn't seem to want to go, even when I rubbed it. As this was still fairly early in the row I became a little concerned as to what might develop, particularly with the constant exposure of my bare feet to the sun. Anyway a few days later I decided to treat myself to a really good wash and after the application of some rather nice smelling Body Shop soapy stuff I realised a miracle had taken place and the red patch had gone. I chuckled to myself, as it dawned on me that rather than developing terminal cancer I had in fact spilt some sauce onto my foot from a packet of Mountain House spaghetti bolognaise (which had very bright red colouring in it) that must have dried before I applied sun block thus sealing it in place! If only cancer cures were so simple!

Chapter Nineteen

February 2004. N24° 05.9' W21° 48.9' – N 16° 18.8' W34° 10.2'

On Monday 2[nd,] as I rowed before sunrise, I noticed a light to starboard. I thought it was probably a distant ship travelling at a fair speed. However I soon realised that this wasn't the case as the light seemed to be fairly steady when visible above the swell and I was slowly overhauling it. I decided to switch on my all round white light so I could be seen and continued on my way. Suddenly there was a bright flash from a torch or searchlight. This caused me to switch on my hand held VHF radio that only had a range of about two miles and I heard a faint voice calling me through the static. It transpired it was Henry Dale aboard 'Kenneth C' with Justin Coleman. It was Henry I spoke to and he said he thought I was 'Kilcullen', the Regatta safety vessel, who, unbeknown to me at the time, was on her way to pick up Justin because he had had enough and couldn't hack it any more. I wished Henry well, turned off the all round white light and rowed on into the dawn contemplating the rather bizarre encounter I had just experienced.

You may be wondering why I turned my navigation light on rather than having it operating during the night. Obviously the idea is to make the boat visible to other vessels but the problem is if you are seen it is likely a large ship will come and investigate. There is probably more danger involved in such a scenario than remaining invisible during the hours of darkness. Most big ships don't keep a weather eye open at night anyway and whilst they are supposed to have a lookout chances are they don't or you won't be seen anyway on account of your relative size. I felt the safer option was to go unnoticed with the light off most of the time and only use it when necessary. This had the added benefit of saving the batteries, loss of power always being of major concern to the ocean rower. The chances of getting run down are very small, nevertheless it remains either the stuff of nightmares or a reality for the few who have had near misses or actually been struck at sea.

On Tuesday, February 3rd, I was entertained by the emergence of a pod of dolphins near the boat, always a welcome sight. This time, however, my first reaction was to shout "Look Josh!" only to realise that of course I was totally alone. I knew my youngest son would have really appreciated watching these amazing creatures going about their maritime business and I felt a bit sad that there was no one with me, as I realised that sharing moments like these are part of what life is all about.

By the 5th I said goodbye to the first 500 miles, however I was becoming increasingly frustrated by the uncooperative wind patterns and by evening it was blowing from the SE. All I could do was attempt to stop the boat going North by pointing the bow to the SW and crabbing almost due West.

The next day the wind was more favourable. I had been rowing for a few hours and at about 0900 hours I saw a large splash some way off the port quarter. I kept looking in the same direction to make sure it wasn't just a large breaking wave and saw a magnificent whale jump clear of the water and crash back into the sea sending up a huge bomb burst of spray. It was awesome, but I was slightly spooked and glad it was some distance off. I was a little on edge for the next 15 minutes or so, in case it came my way and wanted to play! Ships, whales and floating objects like tree trunks and containers that have parted company from ships are all potential hazards for the ocean rower. I remembered reading an article in the *Times* about a couple in Oz who had experienced a whale jumping over their yacht but failing to clear the hull, it landed on top of them, killing itself whilst smashing their vessel, which didn't bear thinking about under present circumstances; perhaps the moral of this was to avoid reading newspapers before an ocean row!

The erratic wind patterns continued. On Saturday, February 7th, I woke at 0200 hours to find the boat subject to an ESE wind crabbing NW! The weather was causing the boat to zig-zag, so rather than congratulating myself on 36 miles of progress in the last 24 hours I was finding it hard to interpret what my actual mileage was directly towards Barbados. This constant uncertainty played havoc with my mental state and I found my mind wrestling with pointless questions. Is there any more I can do? Am I rowing enough? When I'm rowing is it hard enough? Am I eating enough? Is the boat trimmed properly? Will I ever get there? Will the wind ever be more favourable? I realised that I was letting my reaction to the circumstances force me into a downward spiral of mental anguish, I needed to focus on positive things and not let everything get on top of me especially as there was nothing I could do about this damn weather, and feeling like death warmed up wasn't going to help anyone, particularly me! Talking of the weather, I hadn't seen a cloud for a week. Clouds were great friends not only because they gave some respite from the relentless onslaught of the sun's rays but also because they gave perspective to the environment. When the sea was not particularly rough and I sat under a cloudless sky it was like being in the centre of two mighty spheres with nothing to judge distance or perspective, it gave no impression of progress and there was little to gaze upon, I began to understand why the ancient mariner went mad!

On Friday 13th I crossed 20° North and entered the Tropical Zone. I guess this was the point where I believed the NE Trade winds would really kick in and propel me at great speed towards the Caribbean (allegedly!).

Sunday dawned with the promise of a hot day with light winds. I had been doing some filming a few days before with the camcorder in the waterproof bag I had purchased for underwater and bad weather scenarios. The most recent shots were 'cut aways' of the bow slicing through the water. When reviewing this footage I noticed some growth on the underside of the hull and decided I would go over the side, inspect the extent of the problem and clean it off. By the time I was ready to venture forth into the briny depths, the wind had died and it was extremely hot without its cooling influence, probably around 40 degrees centigrade, not uncommon on this route! I checked for sharks, Portuguese Men of War and other unrelated sea monsters and attached myself to the boat with a throw line. I donned a diving mask bought in La Gomera and with paint scraper in hand, lowered myself gingerly into the blue abyss. I was not alone! Four small fish with black and silver vertical stripes that had been my companions for quite some time prior to this inaugural immersion swam around watching the proceedings with great interest. I scraped off various things that had attached themselves over the past few weeks, despite the anti-fouling, inspected the rudder and steering lines and took the opportunity to have a refreshing swim round the boat. It was the first really good wash I had had since departure and it felt great. My only concern at this point was my naked state and the consequences of some creature rising from the deep with the mistaken assumption that a certain part of my anatomy was bait……ouch! In fact looking straight down was a weird sensation, knowing that it was several miles to the seabed and nothing to give any perspective just ever darkening shades of blue as the water got deeper and deeper below me. As I was about to climb back into the boat I noticed something in the water. There were three fish over a metre long swimming round the stern. They were a beautiful blue and yellow with an even brighter yellow 'v' shaped tails. These Dorado or Dolphin Fish as they are known in the Caribbean remained my constant companions for the rest of the journey, being occasionally joined by over 50 others at times…company at last!

By Tuesday, February 17th, I had been at sea for exactly a month. As I rowed ever onward, despite the adverse conditions I contemplated the events of the last week. For no apparent reason I had felt quite down on a couple of occasions and had been fighting back the tears. Even blokes cry sometimes but I felt it important to exert some self-discipline and not allow myself the indulgence as I thought it would take me a while to recover if I let myself be overcome by my circumstances.

It wasn't all doom and gloom however! I had been rowing some exciting seas and particularly enjoyed the experience when there was a good following sea in harmony with a strong wind. It was great fun watching a big wave overtaking the boat, it would get nearer and nearer appearing to gain in height and giving the impression that it would overwhelm the boat. At the last minute the stern would rapidly rise up the face of the wave and as long as it didn't decide to break at that point you would drop over the top and the whole process would start again! Sometimes the wave would break and if I could get the boat lined up properly with good strong stokes on the oars the momentum of the hull at the top of the wave would enable me to surf the boat down the face. Occasionally the wave would break just before I reached the crest and consequently it would dump itself on top of the cabin roof and cover me in spray but that made it even more exhilarating! It was on one of these occasions that the GPS recorded my highest maximum speed to date, of 9.7 knots. I literally shot off the top of a breaking wave and hung on for dear life as the surf boiled along either side of the hull during our speedy descent into the next trough.

I saw my first flying fish. I had seen loads of these in the past but never this close up. I was amazed at how far it managed to glide once it had left the surface of the sea. It was a great novelty at this point in the journey but as I got further South they appeared with greater frequency until they became a welcome but familiar diversion.

I was just short of 1,000 nautical miles out and noted seven end of month facts in my log: -

1. I haven't seen another human being for 4 weeks.
2. The wildlife appearances are moments....otherwise this is a vast and desolate place with ever changing moods.
3. I haven't walked or run for four weeks!
4. I row on and off for 14 hours a day.
5. I live in a space about 4 metres long, cabin for rest and relaxation, cooking and eating area just outside, then the rowing position (think about it!).
6. My mood often depends on the weather: good wind and waves are great, I always want to keep rowing.
7. I eat mainly freeze-dried foods in bags, just add boiling water, they get rather boring.

In fact that Tuesday wasn't great as my log entry revealed and unbeknown to me the prevailing conditions were beginning to set the president for the rest of the journey, I wrote: -

Another poor 24 hours, something I am going to have to get used to over the next week, I think, the forecast is abysmal especially when you consider what it should be. This is what Nayna texted me; Tues 5kns NNE, Wed 5kns NNW, Thurs 10kns NW Fri 10kns NNE….its a nightmare. My main worry is that we go so far south that I won't have enough latitude left to go east. Wind from the North, particularly if it gets stronger, would be a disaster. It's a long way to go but I am continually anxious that I might not reach the island. I just wonder if I am strong enough and have the stamina to do it if these unfavourable conditions continue. If I am not rowing, the boat is drifting slightly east of south which is not helping and who knows what will happen over the next 48 hours if those NW wind predictions are correct.

To cap it all I rowed from 0400 this morning for an hour, stopped for a brew and by 0600 the boat had tracked back along the same course I had just rowed wiping out all that effort, total waste of time and energy. This is getting a bit like the El Hierro experience AND IT'S DAMN HOT!! No clouds and little breeze!!! Oh yes and a hatch handle broke off as well today!!!!

Tuesday, February 17th, wasn't really one of my best days!

However, tomorrow is another day and it gave some cause for celebration as the GPS recorded the completion of the first 1000 nautical miles, but the rejoicing didn't last long as my log records: 'This is outrageous, the wind, what little of it there is has gone round to the West!'

By the afternoon I could not fight it any longer, it had increased to force 3-4 and in order to try and continue the damage limitation with regard to my chosen route, I deployed the Para Anchor for the first time; I just had to sit it out. The wind was literally blowing from the direction in which I wanted to go. By Thursday the wind was blowing hard from the NW, so I spent a fruitless day in the cabin, reading and fretting over my situation. We had been warned that by Friday we could expect some very rough weather that had passed over the Canaries and shut all the ferry services down! I made sure everything was stowed and secure, expecting the worst. At sunset, about 1845 hours, I could see a long line of black clouds coming up over the horizon. There was nothing I could do but stay in the cabin and ride it out. The wind steadily increased as the cloud and rain enveloped me. It was a bit of a fairground ride overnight as this big weather front passed through but we survived even though we had been pushed many more miles to the south. The Para Anchor had been a real Godsend during this period. Deployed over the bow it kept the boat's head to wind and made the ride a whole lot more comfortable, not to mention the fact that it kept the chance of capsize to about nil!

Once the wind subsided, I took the Parachute Anchor in and proceeded to spend a fruitless and exhausting afternoon trying to row West with the wind from the North.

A cloud of indecision enveloped me: should I run with the wind and go yet further South, or re-deploy the parachute and see what happened weather wise? I did the latter.

Saturday was Nayna's birthday, which I celebrated with 'Najojo', Dougan, a tin of Fray Bentos steak and kidney pudding, reconstituted mashed potato, onion and Mountain House French beans, and very nice it was too! One of three Glenfiddich miniatures that she had given me as a leaving present seemed an appropriate way to end the day as I toasted my daughter and the 1,000 miles that now lay behind us with less than 2,000 still to go, or at least that's what I thought at the time!

The wind moderated from the North so I decided to row across it with the waves coming in from the starboard beam. I made reasonable progress, although this kind of situation is a physical and mental killer. On Sunday the wind went into the NE and at noon, when I wrote up the log, I was very surprised to see that I had recorded a distance of 40 nm in the last 24 hours, which under the circumstances was exceptional. I had recorded my feelings on my video diary earlier in the day, recounting how worried I was about the continued drift south and how I had no control over it. The thought of being defeated by the elements was unbearable, as it is those very same elements that I needed to befriend and help me across. I was desperate for consistent ENE or easterly winds. Matt Boreham, another of the solo rowers, was behind me and still further South; I wondered how he was feeling about his situation. Then the wind went back into the North yet again!

I received a text from Usha in the evening to say that solo rower Mark Mortimer had given up, no reasons were given at the time but my heart went out to the guy who must have gone through mental hell to reach that decision.

The following Tuesday, February 24th, at about 0830 hours, I noticed a black blob on the horizon. I couldn't make out what it was at first and then thought it was a sailing vessel tracking the horizon at right angles to me. When you are at sea for as long as I had been you constantly scan the horizon, especially the arc you can see from the rowing position. You get to the point where you almost immediately see anything unusual even when it is very far off. Sometimes this can just be a large wave that rears up a long way off and gives the impression that it is something more substantial, which can be frustrating when you think it could be some kind of object that heralds the promise of human contact. On this occasion, though, the object in question seemed to be on a constant bearing and getting larger. The constant bearing bit meant it was heading for me on a potential collision course. I still thought it was a sailing vessel but decided to get out my binoculars and take a closer look. I could then see it was in fact a cargo ship bows up heading straight for me. It was still some way off but I was aware that from my vantage point, far away wasn't really that far at all and it might be wise take avoiding action. So I turned the boat onto a course at right angles to the ship and rowed like mad for several minutes. The ship was now clearly visible and big! She was some kind of roll on, roll off vessel of about 15,000 tonnes, heading at full speed in the direction I was going. Obviously they hadn't seen me and I saw no one on board, even though they were so close. Like ships that pass in the day, she sped on and I rowed into her wake, just another brief encounter on the briny deep.

I guess the big news on Wednesday was a report from Usha that the first and only fours team in history to embark on an ocean row had arrived in Barbados in 36 days! I wrote in the log: 'What an incredible effort, I must pay tribute to Jason Hart, one of the fours' crew who retired from the 2001 race like me, but unlike me was unfortunate enough to have his boat burnt. To come back and achieve what he has done is brilliant, well done him and the rest of the crew'.

At long long last, on Thursday, the wind went into the ENE blowing about force four, and finally after one and-a-half-weeks I felt that I was beginning to make some progress again in the right direction. In fact the wind direction steadily improved and came round into the East. I was beginning to look forward to reaching the half way point but was aware that I would still have about 1,500 miles to go West, but only 180 South, meaning that I needed to keep going almost due East which was still a cause of some concern, especially after the bizarre wind conditions of the last few weeks.

February therefore ended on a slightly brighter note and my final log entry for the month read: 'I have been rowing in a lively force five easterly wind and the Dorados were jumping this evening when a shoal of about 20 flying fish suddenly appeared out of the water with the setting sun flashing on their silver bodies like diamonds caught in the light. The Darados were chasing them and they were obviously trying to avoid becoming a big fish supper. They looked fantastic!'

Chapter Twenty

March 2004, N16° 23.4' W33° 32.7'– N15° 12.7' W48° 47.4'

The first week of March proved to be the hardest of the trip so far, and probably one of the hardest of my life. Things had been steadily coming to a head in my head and a crisis was looming that ultimately only I could deal with. It is a defining situation that reveals the sort of person you are and whether or not you have the ability to cope in such a harsh environment. Perhaps it is only this kind of extreme circumstance that enables you to find out. Anyway it would be easy for me to give the impression that an ocean row is a doddle and all you have to do is step off the pontoon at the start, row for a few weeks and leave the boat at the other end in a state of euphoria having had the best experience of your life with no real challenges along the way to test your metal. Well if that is the experience of most ocean rowers I am in the minority but, am I bothered?

This is my own unique experience and I want to try and recount it as accurately as possible, because I think it might help others in the future on similar challenges to understand that a row of this kind is a huge undertaking; success is a product of many different factors. Good health, exemplary preparation, fitness, the ability to look after yourself and most of all your courage, determination and ability to keep your head together. All the ocean rowers I have talked to about this say the mental challenge is anything from 75-90% of the challenge. Strangely, it's the area that most of us seem to pay the least attention to when preparing for sea. I guess the reason for this is that nobody really understands what it's going to be like until they are out there and by then it's too late. Upon safe return, perhaps we are inclined to forget the more challenging times and remember the good bits. Or may be it's because nobody has, as yet, come up with a practical and deliverable programme that a potential rower, or team of rowers, can participate in that is of real use when at sea.

The February weather set backs were behind me but just around the corner there was another waiting to bite. On day 42 my GPS recorded 1,504 nautical miles. This was the cause of some celebration on board as I thought it marked crossing the half-way point. I had been really looking forward to this, in fact that would be an understatement, the half way point had become my focus! On that basis I should have made Barbados in 82 days. Prior to leaving many people had asked how long

I thought it would take, what was I aiming for, "65-75 days", I would reply, so clearly this goal was going to be missed!

Most potential rowers will talk about the records they are going to break or the time they expect to be at sea, especially those going out for the first time, trouble is they often haven't consulted Mother Nature, King Neptune or even God about what they might have in mind for the condition of the ocean during the particular period when the potential rower will be at sea. Perhaps the rowers' motto should be 'less blather and more respect'! Not that I have any problem with people trying to break records if that is a motivating factor, but often these predictions are just random guesses based on little substance, except, perhaps, what someone else may have achieved in the past. A lot of that will have been accomplished due to favourable weather conditions, a factor that none of us have any control over.

Anyway to continue the story, I asked Usha on the sat phone to find out from the ORS what in their opinion constituted half way. They said this was achieved by reaching a point 1,435 miles from the island. I checked the GPS again and found that I still had 1752 miles to go which meant I was 300 miles short of half way or at least a week's row if not more! This extra time and distance was probably what we lost as a result of the problems of previous weeks. I was gutted. Then it dawned on me that if it was to take me 10 days to get to the mid-point, which was quite likely if the abysmal weather conditions continued, that would be 52 days in total and potentially another 52 to finish the challenge! The mental pressure was really on!

I think my stress and anxiety had been mounting bit by bit since crossing 20 degrees North on day 25. I now started to go downhill fast, finding it hard to accept my situation. Things just kept going round and round in my head, what if, if only, another 50 days! Not yet half-way, what about those already there, how did they do it, how can Sam and Pavel (two of the other solos) be so far ahead, is my rowing really effective? On and on, round and round, it was like having a tormentor on the boat just telling me I couldn't cope and compared with the rest of the field I was pretty inadequate. Whatever I did I couldn't stop the arguments in my head. Not only did I feel that I had dug a hole for myself, but in trying to get out was only going deeper.

From the outside there was no real reason why I should be like this. I had encountered difficult weather conditions that had split the fleet in half; all those in the front half had kept clear of this and had had generally good conditions to aid their passage. I was at the front of those of us who had got caught and my overall position at that time was half way down the field, which for a solo rower wasn't bad at all. Rationally there was no problem!

On Wednesday, March 3rd, I got on the oars early, even though I felt mentally terrible, but just couldn't row. I was OK physically but just couldn't sum up the mental strength to go on. I was finished and had created a further dilemma for myself as I started to turn over the possible options open to me now. Strangely, giving up wasn't one of them; I guess that would have been too easy!

I had some breakfast and tried again. Then suddenly I had what can only be described as a breakthrough. I dissolved into tears and started to release all the pent up anguish that had been building for so long. I shouted and sobbed like a baby. After a while I began to feel a release and a calm fell upon my soul, I knew it wasn't over but for now I could cope once more, I could go on, I had scaled this unassailable mountain. It was as though I had reached the top only to find another higher, more inaccessible peak ahead of me, which at first sight was just too much, but on reflection I realised I could climb it once I had drunk deep of the strength in the well of my inner being. The key to unlock the entrance to that well had been that moment of utter anguish and despair; in fact it wasn't until then I realised that this hidden inner reservoir of strength even existed. It was something very precious, as I would need to drink deep from its refreshing and life giving waters again and again over the next few weeks.

This may all sound rather poetic but I can only describe it in this manner, it's like reaching the very end of yourself only to find an inner strength that helps you carry on. Rationally I could argue that there were a lot of things that brought me to this point, unrealistic expectations, that 65 - 75 day target being just one. Comparisons with the other rowers in the 'race', something I'll say more about later, and perhaps the utter isolation of it all. I have always maintained that I never felt lonely or alone, but within the inner recesses of my mind perhaps there was a different story being told and the disappointment of thinking I had reached a personal goal that meant a great deal i.e. the half way point, only to realise I still had a long way to go. It was as if the elements were trying to show me how small and insignificant I was against the mighty ocean.

After I had overcome this feeling of utter desolation I spoke to Tim Woodman from the University of Wales. He was a sports psychologist doing a study on all the crews to help people in future events from a psychological perspective. He said I needed to forget past goals and re-appraise my strategy with realistic targets in the light of the experience so far. This was a great help and a practical step forward. In fact the whole journey became a lesson in re-appraisal, even though on every occasion I had to re-appraise my goals downwards, which wasn't fantastically encouraging. When I next spoke to Usha she relayed some wisdom from Tatiana at the ORS who said I needed to ask myself, 'Am I a sportsman and competitor?' If the answer is 'Yes', then I should just get my head down and get across as fast as possible. Or, was I an adventurer who had gone out to participate in something unique that very few others would ever experience? If that was the case I should savour and understand the environment enabling me to return and write about it, sharing the lessons learnt and the awesome nature of the whole expedition. The answer was of course the latter!

She said I should relax, enjoy the experience and not be driven by externals like, my position in the fleet, mileages and unfulfilled and unrealistic goals. She felt I was being robbed of the precious time I had out there alone with nature because of all these pressures and the mental anguish it had caused. Kenneth at the ORS added that I must dig deep and finish the challenge otherwise I would regret it for the rest of my life. Deep down inside I never really thought I would give up, that just wasn't on my agenda despite everything I had endured to date, but I felt all this wisdom was entirely right and as a result I was able to climb back out of the pit of despair and re-establish myself so I could battle on through to the end.

After all this I began to look forward to the half way point. It's all a question of perception. A goal can be something that motivates you but if the position of that goal changes without you recognising it, so you can deal with the consequences, it can become the exact opposite. Becoming de-motivated is a very destructive force and the circumstances surrounding this stage of the trip were teaching me a great deal about this the hard way!

I hope you will allow me to digress for a moment to write a few words about motivation. I believe there is a lot of hog wash on this subject, with a great deal of money lining the pockets of so-called 'Motivational Speakers'. I think it would be more accurate to refer to many of these as 'Verbal Entertainers': people who may have the gift of the gab and entertain their audience but have never motivated anyone. For a start motivation is something that comes from within, I don't believe you can genuinely motivate anyone to do anything, you can ask questions, challenge assumptions, engineer the environment in some cases, you can encourage, empathise and even remonstrate but you will never motivate. Motivation lies within and it is only when you unlock the potential within yourself that you will really accept and rise to the challenge before you. You may listen to advice or have your emotions stirred, you may admire another's achievement or be impressed by the eloquence of a speaker, but it is not until you choose to be motivated by your inner self that anything is really going to happen. It is my contention that circumstances and the environment can be altered to assist that process but the bottom line is that it's up to you to make the choice and act upon it; anything else isn't true motivation in my opinion.

Other factors became important at this stage. Food supplies were one example. I originally took 240 Mountain House Freeze Dried meals, enough for 80 days if I consumed three a day, however I only needed two as I had taken a considerable amount of additional supplies to supplement this. I had Ready Brek mixed with some porridge oats to give it more texture and day bags with crisps, chocolate bars, nuts and other nibbles to keep me going. I also had a daily supply of Biltong, courtesy of my local 'Q' Guild Butcher, Checketts of Ombersley, wonderful stuff! I had plenty for now, but a little voice some way off was warning me that I needed to keep a mental note of what was available in case I had to think about rationing at a later stage.

On Monday, March 8th, I climbed out on deck into a strange light. The sun was merely a red disk in a cloudless sky, unsuccessfully trying to break through a great blanket of red fog. The whole scene felt a bit claustrophobic and I wasn't really sure what was going on. In the end it was the covering of red dust on the boat and wind direction that gave it away. I realised this must be the aftermath of a major dust storm in the Sarah Desert over 1,000 miles to the East.

Dust aside I received a text message from 'Killcullen', the Regatta safety vessel, to say she was making her way up through the fleet and visiting each boat on her way to Barbados. Apparently it was going to be my turn the following day and I was asked to give her a call to check on positions etc, which I did. So Tuesday dawned with a certain sense of anticipation, on the basis that this would be my first human contact for exactly seven weeks, since the start, apart from that rather distant conversation with Henry some way back. Peter Hogden and the crew didn't arrive until 1330 hours, and by that time it was blowing quite hard which meant they couldn't heave to for a chat and instead made about three passes whilst a rather disjointed conversation ensued over the VHF, accompanied by shouts each time they sailed past. Very soon it was all over and they departed to rendezvous with Matt Boreham about 80 miles to the South of my position. The visit was one of mixed emotions. I had felt very excited beforehand at the thought of human contact but the actual encounter had been brief due to the conditions and therefore rather inadequate on the conversational front. By the end of the day I recorded on my video diary that it felt like my personal space had been invaded and I had lost half a days rowing as a result; some people are never satisfied!

The next day I really did make the official half way point although this was never recorded on the ORS website. Usually when an ocean row reaches this point it is recorded on the website by an announcement in red. For some reason this was overlooked in my case and in the end I gave up asking Usha if it had appeared, as after several days I knew I was on the inbound leg despite no official confirmation.

When you live in this kind of environment you become tuned to it and any unusual sound or motion warrants investigation just in case something needs attention. At 0200 hours on Friday, March 12th, I woke to an unusual clunking sound every time the boat rolled. With a force five wind blowing and heavy sea running it was quite hard to move around in the cabin to ascertain the source of the disturbance. In the end I traced it to the upper rudder fastening. I couldn't open the aft hatch because the sea was dumping on the cabin coach roof at regular intervals and as it was dark such a strategy would have ended in a flooded cabin or worse. On further investigation I found a small amount of water leaking into the cabin through the transom, where the bolts fastening a plate to the outside, that supported the upper pintle (rudder fastening), was located. As the boat rolled from side to side the whole plate was moving. The bolts were steadily working loose under the stresses exerted on the rudder and as a result the holes through which they ran were increasing in size, thus letting in the water! After much deliberation I decided to deploy the parachute anchor that would turn the boat into the weather and at first light open the aft hatch and inspect the problem from outside, even though this created a high risk of a heavy sea swamping the cabin.

The little aft hatch on these boats requires you to put an arm through first, followed by the rest of your upper body and turn into a fore and aft kneeling position so you can lean out over the stern. It is quite awkward and in a heavy sea extremely uncomfortable. On inspection I decided a temporary solution was to be avoided as it was obvious that if the whole thing was left too long it would soon lead to the upper fixing being pulled away leaving me rudderless with a big hole in the transom. On inspection I saw that the original bolts were pretty inadequate for the job and so I found some more substantial spares in my tool kit and changed them one by one, with the addition of penny washers and large dollops of marine adhesive to seal them in. It was a hell of a job in such a confined space and meant I had one hand on the outside of the hull holding the end of the bolt with a spanner and the other in the cabin trying to tighten up the nut by touch, as it was impossible to get my head down to see what I was doing due to the angle of the transom and my body filling the hatch, so I could not bend down and see what I was doing. To cap it all I had covered everything in Sikaflex (marine sealing compound) to make sure the repair was watertight and every time I dropped the spanner on the inside of the cabin the compound began to alter the internal décor of the cabin, it was a bit of a mess by the time I had finished! I had my head down most of the time but on the occasions I did look up, a really big swell would tease me as it passed the boat as if to say, 'The next one will swamp you!' Fortunately the Para Anchor did a fantastic job in avoiding that scenario. Once I had completed the job I felt a great sense of satisfaction at having overcome this problem, and the repair I had made seemed to be holding firm.

On the 13th I saw my first and only shark of the journey. In fact I only saw the fin and by the time I got the camera out it was really too far away to register. A couple of days later I celebrated my eldest son John's 20th birthday with the customary steak and kidney pudding and Glenfiddich miniature. Strange to think he had left his teen years behind!

I recorded the best 24 hour run of the trip to date on Wednesday, March 17th, with the expectation that the following day the inbound distance to Barbados would fall below the 1,000 mile mark. I'd be back into three figures!

Sure enough the following day, the GPS recorded only 971 miles to go. This should have been the cause of great rejoicing but alas this milestone was overshadowed by a disaster that threatened bring the whole journey to an abrupt end. An extract from 'Najojo's' logbook for Thursday, March 18th, best describes what happened: -

DISASTER STRUCK, last night the rudder snapped off and now I have no steering gear! I didn't realise this until this morning as the boat went round overnight and I just thought the cleats had popped the steering lines as sometimes happens. I had to go on the oars to get the boat round.

I probably need to give some explanation in this regard. I didn't often row at night and so at the end of each rowing day I would set the boat up to continue in approximately the right direction. This was done by locking the foot steering gear lines in two cleats on either side of the deck, which kept the boat on a more or less straight course, provided the weather was with you. It acted as a very primitive self steering gear. In heavy weather, however, if the boat surfed down a big wave the force exerted on the steering lines would be great enough for the lines to pop out of the cleats, leaving the rudder flapping about until I poked my upper body out of the cabin and re-fastened them. This would generally bring the boat back on course and I could get back to sleep. On this occasion I can only surmise that the lines got jammed and the force on the rudder was so great that it snapped off at water level, rather than the steering lines popping the cleats and thus dissipating the energy. Ironically the repair I had made the previous week held firm, as it did for the rest of the trip! When I re-fitted the boat the rudder and its fitting were the only area I did very little work on as I thought they were probably OK; it just shows how wrong you can be and how *everything* during a boat re-fit should be taken apart, inspected and worked on, especially such an essential piece of equipment.

When the boat was 'running free' at night that sixth sense came into play. I could feel the motion of the boat and as a result knew where the sea was coming from, enabling me to know if I was maintaining the right direction. When the lines popped I would wake almost immediately to address the problem, but if I didn't I would soon wake because I could feel the boat was moving in a different manner, which signified a change of course. If this was left too long then the rudder alone was not enough to get the boat back on course, so I would need to use the oars. That was the case on this occasion and I remember climbing out of the cabin in the dark and trying to pull the boat back onto the right course. I was half asleep and therefore didn't really take much notice of the fact that when I pulled the rudder lines there was no resistance. I guess I just thought I had put things right and went back to sleep.

My Log continues; -

At about 0600 I realised there was more of a problem. I looked over the stern and the top of the rudder looked ok, it was moving as it should be but there was no resistance on the foot steering gear and when it was put full over the boat would not turn. In the end I risked a look through the rear hatch despite the heavy sea and wind and to my horror saw the whole rudder from the metal piece (at sea level) downwards was no longer there. I tried various drogue and rope arrangements but none really worked and cut my speed in half! This scenario could add another five weeks on top of the rest and that's not on! I tried rowing without but the wind just takes you. With wind and sea broadside on you just get pushed sideways. I will try again this afternoon after lunch. This is really the final straw! I am so gutted, I did about the best mileage ever yesterday and everything was looking good for Barbados in about four - five weeks, less at the current rate, now it could all end in nothing. Stein Hoff called and advised me to put as much weight aft as possible and see if that would help.

My initial thoughts centred on whether or not I could continue and I probably needed to take stock of the situation and give myself time to see if I could do without a rudder and consider any possible solutions to the problem. By the end of the day I was exhausted and decided to sleep on it. I had deployed a small drogue and found that it had kept me reasonably well on course. Early the next morning, before first light, I got up to tend the lines and consider what next. I had put on my all round white light so I could see what I was doing and noticed the navigation lights of a ship some way off. I carried on minding my own business but realised the ship was coming towards me. It got pretty close and suddenly a blaze of light shone in my eyes as a searchlight was pointed in my direction. I had switched on my handheld VHF and a voice with a heavy Spanish accent asked if I wanted any help. Imagine the scene, a cargo ship going about its business some 1,500 miles from land and comes across a little yellow boat with a single bloke and a big beard; I could understand the slight tinge of incredulity in his voice! I declined his offer, unless he could construct me a new rudder, but I don't think he understood what I was on about. I said goodbye and wished him a good journey. I heard the engines accelerating and soon he was no more than a light on the horizon. This presented an ideal opportunity for me to have abandoned the whole thing, especially as it was so close to the loss of the rudder, but it underlined my determination not to give up.

Over the next few days I noticed that although I was able to row without the rudder my mileage had been cut in half. Some days I was doing less than 20 miles towards the island and, to cap it all, Matt Boreham, finally overtook me, leaving me in his wake to arrive some 20 days ahead of me in the end! Louise Ginglo, Henry Dale, Sally and Sarah Kettle were still behind me, but without the loss of the rudder I could well have got in about the same time as Matt.

A flood of text messages from home encouraged me; the sense of people willing me on was almost tangible. I celebrated Joshua's birthday on 20th followed by mine on 22nd. I wrote in my log, 'It's my birthday and the sad git's on his own for a change'. The bright point of this day was the boat appearing to pick up some speed. I had spoken to Sam who by now was in Barbados having won the solo element of the Regatta. He said that once he got down to 14 degrees, 30 minutes North, he had picked up some kind of current that had propelled him towards the island to such an extent that on a couple of days he didn't even bother to row! I was beginning to experience the same effect now that I had crossed 15 degrees North and was hoping it would increase as I tracked South.

On 24th I had a strange encounter. I was rowing along in a fairly calm sea when a long way off to starboard I could hear what sounded like rushing water. As I looked in the direction it was coming from I saw what I can only describe as great plumes of water emanating from the surface of the sea. If you can imagine it looked like the effect when a World War Two plane fired its guns into the water, sending up two tracks of spray as the shells hit the surface and it was coming towards me fast! I dived for the camera and by the time I had it ready to roll realised that this was a pod of some 30+ dolphins swimming at great speed in my direction. I didn't get any good footage, though, as they dived before getting that close to the boat and were gone forever.

On the 25th I decided to apply myself to resolving the rudder situation one final time. I suddenly realised that the top part above the point at which the wood had snapped at water level was still lodged between the two metal fixing plates holding the whole thing in place. I had taken all this off the stern earlier in the week and, contrary to my original supposition that the lower bracket had gone with the rudder, both brackets were still in place. If I could get the wood out from between these plates and find another suitable piece to attach it to there was a small chance I could cobble something together that might just work! I searched around the boat for the umpteenth time and it suddenly dawned on me that the gunwale at the old forward rowing position had re-enforced undersides and if I could cut that out it might just do the trick. I only had a Stanley saw and was concerned I would snap the blade as it cut through layers of ply and epoxy. After a great deal of effort the piece came away, I had to be careful because the plastic tube that carried the forward solar panel cables back to the cabin ran underneath where I was cutting. After pulling the original piece of rudder from between the metal rudder fixing plates, I shaped the top of the piece I had cut from the boat, covered it in a thick layer of Sikaflex sealant and drilled some bolt holes, breaking the hand drill in the process! I applied more gunk and took the top section of the old rudder I had just removed from the plates, inverted it and screwed it to the bottom of the new section. Once all this was done it didn't look pretty but it did look as though it might work. I left it to go off a bit in the sun then went over the side to rig the steering lines, watched by at least eight big Dorados. I came back aboard and rigged the jury rudder from the aft hatch, securing everything in place. It was late evening by this time and I was absolutely exhausted, the first trial for the 'new' rudder would have to wait until the morning.

On Saturday, March 27th, the sea seemed to speed up. I know this sounds strange but it is the only way I can describe it. I had been trying hard to get further South to 14 degrees 30ish, where Sam had said he picked up this current that took him all the way to the island. The real change came at 14 degrees 50 minutes South, and I felt elated as for once things seemed to be going in my favour. By the following day I had recorded a distance of 39 nm in the last 24 hours, which was great, and the jury rudder not only seemed to be holding up but doing the job it was designed for with great efficiency. Perhaps my luck was changing!

Left: The author had to cut up the gunwale so as to repair the broken rudder.

Right: The author then cut up the old forward reinforced rowing position to create a makeshift rudder.

Left: The author displays the jury rudder upon arrival in Barbados.

Chapter Twenty-one

April 2004, N15° 20' W49° 05' – N14° 42' W59° 26.3'

By now I had 20-30 Dorado as my constant companions. They were very active, regularly jumping out of the sea to chase and catch the poor old flying fish in spectacular style. They also had the habit of rubbing themselves along the hull, the sound of which was a little disconcerting at first.

Dougan appeared to have organised an April Fool with them, as early on April 1st I used my trusty plastic bed pan and threw it over the side for its usual flush. Unfortunately the lanyard that had held it all the way to that point had come undone and the whole thing disappeared forever! Was it my imagination or could I hear Dougan saying "April Fool" and laughing as the Dorado jumped around the boat to the distant sound of sub aquatic laughter! Good job I had a spare bucket!

Whilst I'm engaged in these random musings I had had plenty of time to observe the antics of the wildlife and noted some points on the behaviour of Dorado. I noted these magnificent creatures regularly made three kinds of jumps that I named, the slap, the high dive and the terminator! The slap is the most common, when the fish comes out of the sea just above the surface on its side, slapping it with its tail or the whole of its body, generally done in a series of two or three. The high dive is the most spectacular when done with finesse. The fish launches itself from under the surface into the air and then comes down on its side with a big slap and splash. When they do this from the top of a wave they can propel themselves from eight - 10 feet into the air. It's brilliant! They generally do this once or twice. Finally the Terminator, it's very fast and they jump out of the water upright rather than on the side with great speed. It's done when chasing flying fish and I've seen up to three Dorado in pursuit of one fish. They can swim and jump as fast as the poor old flying fish can fly! The end result is inevitable. It all provided endless excitement and entertainment.

One afternoon I observed four or five shoals of flying fish with several hundred in each, leaping out of the water in different directions. It was mayhem as the Dorados went in for the kill. There were also a couple of birds dive-bombing them, a truly amazing spectacle.

By the 2[nd,] wildlife aside, I was 'shedding tears of frustration'. As I said before the current had picked me up as I worked my way steadily south. However, as soon as I got into an ideal position the wind went into the South, pushing me relentlessly North, back over latitudes I had only recently crossed in the other direction. Fortunately I was able to maintain a bit of West, which was vaguely encouraging. I had been totally becalmed during the previous 24 hours and by the evening the boat was lazily going round in circles!

I was woken at 0430 hours the next morning by the sound of a breeze so decided to get on the oars. As I rowed I saw I was dropping due South again! However this was short lived as the wind had been created under local cloud, soon going back into the South and dying as the cloud moved on. With no wind and no cloud the sun's heat was oppressive and I had to throw water on the deck just so I could stand on it without burning my feet. At noon I recorded a 24 hour run of 19nm, the worst of the trip so far! I had been told that after the half way point conditions would improve and it would be all down hill from there; was this someone's idea of a joke? If so, I can't say that I appreciated their sense of humour! Mine, on the other hand, emerged occasionally, such as when I wrote in the log 'By the way, if anyone knew an easier way of getting to Barbados, why on earth didn't they tell me!'

The weather forecast for the previous week had been good, winds from the E or ENE but in reality it remained constantly S-SE. In fact the weather forecasting had been totally unreliable for weeks. It's something you end up trying to ignore because it continually brought the promise of good winds in the right direction, but the reality was always different, generally unfavourable and consistently wrong! I think this was because they came as a prediction from weather models on computers and bore very little relation to reality. It was only towards this last part of the journey that a friend of mine in Worcester started to get involved that things on this front (if you'll pardon the pun!) began to improve.

Saturday 3rd was a fascinating day from a weather perspective. The most incredible cloud formations moving in different directions with an awesome multi-coloured sunrise!

To get away from the vagaries of the weather, as I think you will have got the general idea by now that the NE Trade Winds are probably a figment of someone's imagination or should be re-named the SE Trades in these latitudes, I wrote an interesting piece in one of my weekly updates, as I think people were beginning to show some concern that I wasn't enjoying the experience at all.

I wrote: -

In 1999 I gave my Dad a book called 'Finest Hour'. I decided to take it on the boat and have just finished reading it. It records the war year of 1940 through the eyes of ordinary people, it is fascinating, harrowing in parts but captures the intensity of those desperate times. Dad talked a lot about the war years and for him the friendships, action and intensity of the experience was something he saw as a defining moment in his life.

Usha had a conversation with someone recently who said they felt it was a shame I hadn't enjoyed the whole experience of this row more. This started me thinking about the nature of it and what exactly the word 'enjoy' meant. Now stay with me on this one! The analogy of a punnet of strawberries came to mind. Every year about June time we go up the road in Worcester and pick strawberries. We bring them home and eat them, it's an enjoyable if brief seasonal experience. However with a lot more effort, expense and time we can preserve the fruit and flavours by turning the strawberries into jam. OK the end product is somewhat different from the fresh variety but the flavour is intense and if you make enough it is there in the cupboard to enjoy whenever you like. We can all recall times in our lives when we have had momentous and sometimes life changing experiences and often they are the result of difficulties or dangers that have brought out the best in us and others and therefore been preserved in our memory to be drawn on in the future a bit like the jam! They become part of us and our existence and we become far richer through perseverance and facing the challenges along the way.

When I left La Gomera 11 weeks ago I really didn't know what to expect, I knew the experience would be enjoyable, intense, challenging, pretty awful at times as well as moments of peace and satisfaction mixed with loneliness and may be even pain. It has been all of these and much much more besides. If I had left the island and sung sea shanties all the way to Barbados, got off the boat and got on with life it might have been an enjoyable and fun experience but probably had little impact on me as an individual and my future life. So far this experience has been like turning those fresh strawberries into jam and when I get to the end the whole process of creating those intense flavours and having them with me to draw on for the rest of my life is really what this journey is all about. Ultimately the harsh nature of this challenge will be the thing I have enjoyed the most because that will be the thing that I have overcome and learnt from. Perhaps a lot of my reports from out here have given the impression I'm not that happy with my lot, I guess it's those moments that get reported if daily news is anything to go by. The fact is if I hadn't done this I wouldn't be able to capture the deep things I have been learning about myself. War is a dreadful thing but if the accounts of "Finest Hour" are anything to go by the sheer intensity and nature of the experience brings about unique and positive human attributes alongside all that is awful about conflict, much of which is far from enjoyable for those involved. Jam preserves the nature of fresh fruit and prolongs its life for the enjoyment of others for a great deal longer than the strawberry season. I have enjoyed these experiences so far and I have been ground down (in a positive sense) for eleven weeks. I know my memory of this row will be preserved and my life won't be the same again. I think I am going to enjoy the fruit of my hard won success perhaps I'll even see it as my 'Finest Hour'.

The mental and physical challenges continued on into April. I won't go into too much detail, as I would end up with a long list of adverse wind directions and weird currents. Suffice to say that my log entry for Easter Day Sunday, April 11th, sums up most of what had been going on for the previous week: -

The sound of the wind woke me at 0200 hours. The boat was going slightly east of north and there was nothing I could do about it. At 0600 hours I had breakfast and tried various things to stop the run north. Rowing only enables me to get the boat slightly west of north, which isn't worth the effort. Deploying the parachute anchor takes the boat due east which is probably as bad as due north and the smaller drogue did the same. So I am just going to have to sit it out! I am getting a bit fed up with all of this! 13 miles North and – five miles East! The pits. This weather has got to change otherwise I am stuffed!! It is now day 81 and I am back at the same latitude as on day 60, March 20th! Deployed Para Anchor again:

At   1400 N15° 33.3' W52° 27.7'
by   1600 N15° 33.7' W52° 26.3' = 0.4 nm north & 1.5 nm east
by   1800 N15° 34.2' W52° 24.8' = 0.5 nm north & 1.5 nm east

And so the drift continued. By noon the following day I recorded 23 miles in the wrong direction!

At midnight on Monday the wind went into the North so I retrieved the Para Anchor that I had been on for about three days, trying to stop myself loosing ground to the weather. I started rowing at 0530 hours with the wind slowly going into the NE. I had probably lost at least 100 miles towards Barbados over the previous week.

Basically the wind went into the South on March 25th, driving me relentlessly North and it stayed there despite contrary forecasts and the promise of change until April 16th! During this time I had also been pushed back East but had managed to limit the damage by use of the Para Anchor. I was completely becalmed twice and rowed up and down the same patch of ocean four times. Each time I thought I'd get back South only to be blown back North. It was a nightmare! The outcome of all this has been a huge circle that has taken me back to the same position as 10 days before.

Now, for the first time in four weeks, I was beginning to enjoy a row that was weather assisted, even though the wind needed to settle down properly from the East and by this time I had very little confidence that it would. It seemed unlikely I would make land fall in Barbados because by now I was so far North. If I got a consistent and constant NE wind there was an outside chance I might make it to land.

It seemed an appropriate time to get poetic and so I penned two pieces that seemed to sum up the present situation. The first tries to convey the wretched experience when becalmed: -

Waiting for the Wind

Undulating silence under a burning sun
Unable to determine any compass point
Directionless, suffocating,
Halting progress
When will it end?
When will my heart be at peace through movement?
Sun baked time stands despairingly still
Oh for the cool of evening
Oh for the wind of motion
Oh for the south to turn to east
Oh for the island destination.

This next poem, 'All Down Hill' was a bit more tongue in cheek: -

It's all down hill from half way
That's what the people said
I'm not so sure I would agree
In fact I feel mislead
Today we're going to the east
With winds up from the south
Tomorrow we'll go to the north
We could end up in Louth!
Or else I'll just go round and round
Waiting for a change
It could go on forever
As I become deranged
The sun is trying to cook me
At night I watch the moon
I wonder if I'll still be here for hurricanes in June!
I could be an attraction for a Caribbean cruise
The ship could come and circle round
While all the people muse

On what it must be like to row
Upon the briny deep
With minimal progression
And not a lot of sleep
I'm out in the Atlantic
With not a lot of hope
Perhaps I need a bit of prayer
Could someone call the Pope!
If ever I get out of this
At least there'll be some cheer
Of welcoming the bailiffs
With a nice cold glass of beer
This story has a moral
For those who wish to row
It's easier on the Serpentine
And not so far to go!

The weather situation was still confused but by the 16th it was beginning to show signs of assisting me. By now, though, I wasn't about to trust it for five minutes! A guy called Dave Cave who I knew in Worcester had come on the scene during this final part of the journey. He had been brilliant in sending me weather forecasts that were generally correct and giving me a lot of moral support. He was well aware that food could become a problem, particularly if I missed Barbados completely and had to head for another island further North, which was looking a distinct possibility as 'Kilcullen' had a limited range regarding a tow. From the 16th, therefore, we devised a grid with eight columns as follows: -

- Day, position, Distance from 59° 37' W (the official finish longitude which runs through the north point of Barbados).
- Distance travelled in the last 24 hours on the GPS.
- Days to the line calculated from the last 24 hour run.
- Number of days food left.
- Days of food left minus days to the line.

This became a really useful measure of not only how much food remained but also how well I was doing regarding progress to the finish line.

The next week was characterised by a relentless push for the finish line. I noted in the log that Kenneth at the ORS was sending me text messages on a number of occasions to tell me to get South. It's so easy when you are outside the situation to interpret what is going on at sea wrongly. I knew Kenneth had my best interests at heart and in the following days after reaching the island I became only too aware of the stress on those waiting for the next boat to arrive. I understood there was a lot of discussion going on with regard to whether or not 'Kilcullen' would be able to meet me and if not which island I should be instructed to head for, but my problem was that I had no control over the elements and until the wind and current decided to give me a break I couldn't row against it. I was just going further and further North. Now things were beginning to look up and I was starting to be able to claw my way South, little by little until Sunday 25th!

My log entry read thus: -

Wind went SE at 0400 and remained there most of the morning causing me a great deal of stress. Managed to keep roughly west but across wind and waves, very anxious moments as I thought the wind might set in again especially as Usha and Josh are flying out from the UK tomorrow! Came round into the east again about 1100 hrs but lots of heavy cloud and showers around creating their own local weather.

A huge mass of cloud came over after a couple of really good hours of east force 4 it sucked me under it and I am now being driven north again. I'm in the cabin with torrential rain hammering on the deck head. It's the heaviest rain of the trip so far. This is so frustrating I am only 130 nm from Barbados and was going so well south after loosing so much to the north over past weeks. Dave Cave just rang and is on the case weather wise. He rang back to say he had looked at the satellite photo of the area where I am and he could see a large area of cloud over my position but the rest of the Atlantic right back to the Cape Verdi islands was clear! He didn't think it would last long so hold tight, have some food and get some rest!

'A huge mass of cloud came over...'

Visitors taking a rest from the bad weather.

BBC Hereford & Worcester Radio had been in contact with home and asked if they could interview me live on the breakfast show at 0700 hrs BST, but the only trouble was this was 0200 hrs my local time. Anyway always up for a challenge I did the earliest live breakfast interview ever!

By Tuesday 27th and despite all efforts I was still going North. I had been on the phone a couple of times to Sally and Sarah Kettle, the mother and daughter team who were the next boat back from me, with Louise Ginglo in 'Moose on the Move' and Henry Dale in 'Kenneth C' bringing up the rear. It was great to talk to them, the empathy was amazing as we all understood exactly what we had to endure, all were so encouraging. At 1600 hours Dave predicted that it would be another 12 hours before the wind came round to ENE and then the sea should settle down too. He suggested that I rest and wait…..I had heard that somewhere before!

After some time I made a closer inspection of the GPS. Zooming in to maximum magnification I noticed that I was on a reciprocal course, going back almost exactly South along the same track I had previously been tracking North! My progress had finally ended 95 miles north of Barbados.

By now the sea was very intimidating for some reason but I was able to make steady progress South and West. On Thursday, April 29th, I got on the oars and rowed for 24 hours, only stopping for food and drinks. The wind was assisting me South, and it steadily came further and further round into the North. This had two advantages: it meant I was getting closer to the island from the North and closer to the line to the West. 'Kilcullen' had left Barbados to rendezvous with me as soon as

I had crossed the official finish longitude. The debates about whether or not I was too far North had ended when they realised how fast I was suddenly dropping South.

I rowed steadily on through the night. By now the wind was pushing me almost due South. I was getting closer and closer to the line, but even in these final moments of the voyage there was a sting in the tail. I had to track the boat across the wind to get to the line. My progress South was amazing but by now it was very hard to make any way West. The sun was rising on April 30th, day 100, and I had rowed for four hours, only making half a mile West! I was only 70 miles North of Barbados and exhausted. The finish line was only about three nm away to the West, but it could have been 300. I decided to rest but thought this futile, as it was already light and getting hotter by the minute. I remember staring at the clock on the cabin bulkhead thinking I wouldn't sleep, when I looked again having no recollection of time, it was two hours later! I went out on deck and the wind had come round a little, enabling me to get on the oars and row the final couple of miles over the line.

At 0951 local time on Friday, April 30th, 2004, the GPS read N14° 33.483' W59° 37.092' with a total mileage of 3,439 nautical miles.

Dougan, 'Najojo' and I had done it! I had rowed the Atlantic Ocean solo! The toughest challenge of my life had come to an end! Or had it?

Chapter Twenty-two

I experienced a cocktail of emotions when crossing the finish line: relief, excitement, anticipation in the knowledge that this monumental project I had lived with for over six years was now complete. However, there was little time for circumspection; I needed to concentrate on securing the boat in anticipation of the arrival of 'Kilcullen' for the tow back to Barbados. The fact that I hadn't actually made landfall was disappointing, but the 'rules' of the Regatta, in line with previous events, stated that crossing W 59° 37', the line of longitude running through the North Point of Barbados, marked the end of an Atlantic Crossing on this route, and I wasn't about to argue with that! Anyway, given the foul conditions I had experienced for so much of the voyage it would have been impossible to have done anything else. In fact it was a bit of a miracle that I ended up only 70 miles North of the island, since the conditions of only a week or so earlier could have taken me at least 300 miles further North if they hadn't abated!

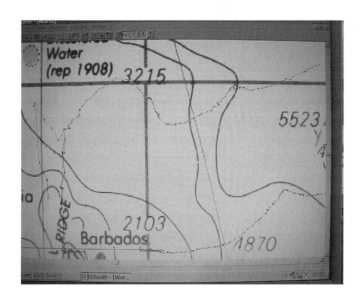

Computer screen on 'Kilcullen' tracking my progress to the RV, 75 miles North of Barbados.

After a short while 'Kilcullen' hove in view, although she was almost alongside before Peter and the crew saw me, a stark reminder of how small and insignificant I was out there and a fact accentuated once I was aboard the yacht when I looked back to see how tiny 'Najojo's' hull looked on the end of the tow. Phil was kneeling in the rubber dinghy, attached by a line to 'Kilcullen'; as it bumped into the side of 'Najojo', I leapt in, having secured the tow line, and we were both unceremoniously hauled back to the yacht. There I received an enthusiastic

Phil & the author prepare to board 'Kilcullen'.

The author leaves 'Najojo' for the tow to Barbados.

welcome as we began the last leg to Port St Charles. I was exhausted and spent a great part of the trip asleep. Eventually Barbados came into view and I watched the West coast of the island slip by in the dark as we made our way to Port St Charles. Past the cement works and fishing traps until we rounded the breakwater at 0200 hours on May 1st, after 101 days and 19 hours at sea.

Usha, Josh and my Mum appeared a bit later, after first light. It was great to see them again and feel the warm embrace of those you love. I had to prepare the boat for transportation back to the UK but after that we spent a relaxing week on the island before leaving for home.

I received a great welcome from many local people who had lived the journey with me, through the weeks and months from news and my weekly reports. With their help we had raised £20,000 for St Richard's Hospice over the whole duration of the project. The media had been very supportive throughout and ran various articles drawing a line under the events of the last few years.

Once I had returned home I knew that I would feel some kind of hole in my life but didn't realise just how much of a challenge this would be. It took between six months and a year to really feel a sense of closure on the whole thing, but I felt there was a window of opportunity to develop presentations around all aspects of the row and to push open a number of other doors that where beginning to appear on the horizon. So on November 1st, 2004, I left the Worcestershire Youth Service and became self-employed.

So ended the final chapter of my great ocean adventure. A new a very different challenge lay before me as I made the first tentative steps into the unknown territory of self-employment. The future promised to hold new challenges of a very different nature, but the experience of the mighty Atlantic Ocean had taken me to a higher level of self-belief that would set me in good stead to make the best of whatever lay ahead.

Finishing this book has taken a long time, partly because of the demands of work but also because it took a while before I was ready to re-visit my logs, journals and other materials. It took time to get over the feeling that a lot of ocean rowers seem to reflect on completion of a major project, one apparently shared by women who have just given birth and say "Never again", only to find a short while later another one is on the way!

As for me, plans are beginning to take shape for another huge rowing project. Whether or not they will finally come to fruition depends on a number of things, not least of which will be proper sponsorship. Unless you have embarked on this kind of adventure it is hard to realise just what an enormous commitment is involved. I had to hold down a demanding full time job, raise the funds to do the trip as well as those allocated to the Hospice, build a boat the first time round, refit the second, do all the necessary research, bearing in mind my life might depend on getting it right, engage in long and demanding training programmes, procure all the necessary equipment, learn how to use it and a whole lot more besides. I really enjoyed the whole experience even though it was the toughest thing I have ever done in my life. I can use this expertise for the future but decent sponsorship has to be the way to go in order to dedicate the kind of time needed for success and to fulfil the project's maximum potential.

The question people ask the most about the voyage is "Why"? So perhaps I will leave the last word with the first man to row an ocean solo. John Fairfax completed his 180-day Atlantic row in 1969, and when asked why he said:

"The quest to prove worthy of an almost inconceivable challenge is our greatest reward"

www.rowextreme.com

In the great British traditions of seafaring and exploration, the author is currently planning his next venture, The World Row Challenge: 20,000 miles on the edge of endurance in one of the world's most inhospitable environments.

After his successful 2004 solo Atlantic row, Worcester based Expedition Leader Richard Wood has turned his attention to attempting a world first: rowing round the world without making landfall. This will be achieved in a custom-built Ocean 4 rowing boat with a crew of three for each ocean leg of the voyage, enabling each crewmember to join those exclusive individuals who have rowed an ocean.

The expedition's Pacific leg is scheduled to depart Australia in 2007. After re-supply and crew change off South America, the Atlantic leg will then take place. Having completed the second and final re-supply and crew change off South Africa, the Indian Ocean leg will bring the voyage to a conclusion back in Oz. Richard will remain on board to lead the expedition throughout the voyage, which is expected to last 10 months.

Richard says "This is the opportunity of a lifetime for nine individuals to join me in attempting a truly awesome challenge. Success will place this expedition in the ranks of outstanding human achievement".

Richard will be charting the passage of this truly remarkable challenge in his second book *The Edge of Endurance*.

St. Richard's Hospice

CARING FOR LIFE

St Richard's Hospice has been caring for over 22 years for thousands of patients and families in Worcestershire who are living with cancer and other life-threatening illness.

Staff and more than 600 dedicated volunteers provide specialist care and support through a wide-range of free services, including a Day Hospice, Home Care Team, Bereavement, Social Work, Family Therapy & Counselling Service, 24-hour On Call Advice Line and The Snowdrop Group for your young women living with cancer. Each year around 1,500 patients and bereaved families are supported by the Hospice.

In 2006, thanks to generous backing from the community, the new £5.25m St Richard's Hospice opens to patients, offering all the current services and 15 desperately needed specialist beds, the first of their kind in South Worcestershire. The Hospice is independant and needs to raise the majority of its running costs through voluntary donations.

To make a donation or for more information, please contact: -

St Richard's Hospice
Rose Hill
London Road
Worcester WR5 1EY
Tel: 01905 763963
Fax: 01905 351911
www.strichardsorg.uk
Charity No: 515668

Your Memories in Print?
Your Book Published?

**VICTORY
BOOKS**

**VICTORY
BOOKS**

We can make YOUR idea a REALITY in print!

Victory Books was founded in 2005 by well-known and successful author & specialist publisher Dilip Sarkar MBE, whose new vision builds upon the succes of his previous operation, Ramrod Publications (1992-2002). Just one year later, Victory Books is already a thriving partnership, owned by the Sarkar and Cooper families, based in Worcester, UK, publishing books from many authors on an equally diverse range of subjects.

For example, concurrently with this book, Victory has released *Spitfire! Courage & Sacrifice* by Dilip Sarkar, and Fred Roberts' wartime memoir *Duxford to Karachi: An RAF Armourer's War.* 2006 will also see release of books such as Dr Bernard-Marie Dupont's paper on palliative care, and internationally renowned sculptor Kenneth Potts' book promoting his work.

Victory Books therefore invites submissions on any subject, from new or established authors, and can provide a bespoke service to suit each individual. Services offered range from general evaluation of material, editing, layout, print and bind, and often Victory Books will also deal with marketing, promotion and distribution on the author's behalf.

To see your work in print, or for more information, please contact the Commissioning Editor at Victory Books who will personally give professional advice and outline a bespoke package that will make your idea a reality in print.

Victory Books, PO Box 573, Worcester WR5 3RU, UK
Tel: 07921 503105   Fax: 01905 767735
www.VictoryBooks.co.uk   info@victorybooks.co.uk